PRAISE FOR

SPIRITUAL HOUSECLEANING

❖

Hosea 4:6 says, "My people are destroyed for lack of knowledge."
Alice and Eddie Smith share prophetic and practical truths
that will bring greater freedom for you and your family.
I highly commend this outstanding book.

DR. CHÉ AHN
President, Harvest International Ministries
Senior Pastor, Harvest Rock Church
Pasadena, California

Many things in the world today that are called faddish are a
fetish. God has opened the eyes of Eddie and Alice Smith's
understanding to teach us on how to keep these things out of
our homes. Open your hearts to this book's message and enjoy!

KIMBERLY DANIELS
Bestselling Author of *Give It Back!* and *Inside Out*

Spiritual Housecleaning is a timely message to the Body of
Christ, calling us all to a new level of holiness. We have left
open spiritual doors to the enemy in our homes, churches
and hearts. Alice and Eddie Smith have given us the keys
to free ourselves from demonic hindrances that have
infiltrated our walk with God.

FRANCIS FRANGIPANE
Author, *The Three Battlegrounds*
Senior Pastor, River of Life Ministries
Cedar Rapids, Iowa

The Bible admonishes us to "leave no [such] room or foothold for the devil [give no opportunity to him]" (Eph. 4:27, *AMP*). Eddie and Alice Smith show how, through our ignorance and carelessness, the devil can take advantage of us through things in our possession. From Scripture and personal experience, they enlighten us on the importance of spiritual housecleaning and how to go about it.

FRANK D. HAMMOND
Author, *Pigs in the Parlor* and *A Practical Guide to Deliverance*

Eddie and Alice Smith and their book *Spiritual Housecleaning* have managed to capture with great insight issues that plague many people because of historical and spiritual violations on people's land prior to them purchasing it. This can include their houses. I believe this book to be essential in understanding how spiritual powers work and how to combat those forces and ensure God's presence.

JOHN PAUL JACKSON
Streams Ministries International

Spiritual Housecleaning is a practical tool for every believer committed to living a holy and free life! I have personally seen people around the world bring hundreds of items to an altar of repentance to break their ties with sin. I highly recommend this book, as it is written by qualified servants of the Lord, Eddie and Alice Smith, who have accumulated a wealth of experience on the subject for over 30 years. This book is a gift from God to the Body of Christ around the world, offering teaching and instruction on how to finally keep our homes and lives free of any spiritual trash.

SERGIO SCATAGLINI
Author, *The Fire of His Holiness*
President, Scataglini Ministries, Inc.

Satan and the forces of evil do everything they can to discourage the Christian—including attempting to invade our homes. This is part of the conflict in the invisible world. We must be aware of and cut off the subtle ways Satan trespasses and attempts to rob us of blessings right where we live. Eddie and Alice Smith point us to the place where we must begin— in our own souls and homes. They show us how to cleanse our attitudes and every physical room where we reside. The Smiths give us a step-by-step guide to taking unlimited authority over demons and reclaiming our homes for the Lord. They show us how to apply the biblical truth that in God's wonderful order, "He who is in you is greater than he who is in the world" (1 John 4:4).

PAT ROBERTSON
Host, *The 700 Club*
Founder and Chairman, The Christian Broadcasting Network

If we are ignorant of the wiles of the devil, he will surely take advantage of us. With *Spiritual Housecleaning*, Eddie and Alice Smith have exposed his wiles and dealt a severe blow to the kingdom of darkness. This book will help you break satanic bondages and set you free for victory!

C. PETER WAGNER
Chancellor, Wagner Leadership Institute
President, Global Harvest Ministries
Colorado Springs, Colorado

spiritual
HOUSECLEANING

Protect Your Home and Family from Spiritual Pollution

REVISED AND UPDATED

New
Amazing
Stories of
Victory

Eddie & Alice smith

Regal

From Gospel Light
Ventura, California, U.S.A.

Published by Regal
From Gospel Light
Ventura, California, U.S.A.
www.regalbooks.com
Printed in the U.S.A.

Disclaimer: Please exercise caution and wisdom before destroying antiques, furniture,
jewelry and other things that have monetary value. The Holy Spirit should direct
everything we do as we spiritually clean our homes. Colossians 3:15 reminds us:
"And let the peace of God rule in your hearts."

Library of Congress Cataloging-in-Publication Data
The Library of Congress has catalogued the first edition as follows:
Smith, Alice
Spiritual housecleaning / Alice and Eddie Smith.
p. cm.
Includes bibliographical references.
ISBN 0-8307-3107-5
1. Spiritual warfare. I. Title: Spiritual house cleaning. II. Smith,
Eddie. III. Title.
BV4509.5 .S62 2003
235'.4—dc21

Rights for publishing this book outside the U.S.A. or in non-English languages are
administered by Gospel Light Worldwide, an international not-for-profit ministry.
For additional information, please visit www.glww.org, email info@glww.org, or write
to Gospel Light Worldwide, 1957 Eastman Avenue, Ventura, CA 93003, U.S.A.

CONTENTS

❖

PART ONE:
spiritual Housecleaning principles

PART TWO:
stories and Applications

❖

FASTEN YOUR SEATBELTS

In the 1980s, I (Eddie) took a church pastoral staff job, and we bought a house and settled down. Alice became an award-winning real estate agent. During the next 11 years, we served a local congregation in Houston, Texas. It wasn't long before we encountered experiences with the demonic among our membership, and then other churches began to send us people who needed counseling involving the supernatural, demons and the rest.

One night, we facilitated the deliverance of a dear lady in northwest Houston. To make an extremely long story short, we and another pastor from our church were challenging the demons that were tormenting the lady when we asked, "What gives you the right to stay in her?"

With that, the lady's arm involuntarily moved above her head and pointed to a bookshelf with a sliding door. We opened the door and discovered a "Christian" book about demons. "This?" we asked.

The lady's face twisted into a sarcastic sneer, and the demon (speaking through her) said devilishly, "Yes."

Without a thought, I ripped the book into shreds. As I did, the demons shrieked and left her. She was freed.

Our pastoral team learned to minister to people using ministry teams of three to five people. Soon, we had developed a system we called Ministry Team Training to teach our church members how to minister in teams. Before long, hundreds of people from churches across the South came to our church to be trained at our quarterly training events. The course further developed as the experience of our team grew. Soon we had established multiple levels of training.

Shortly after leaving the church to do the work we now do— writing and teaching at conferences around the world—we wrote the original edition of *Spiritual Housecleaning*. To our amazement (and perhaps our publisher's!), our book became an overnight bestseller. People from various nations, cultures and languages sent us praise reports. They'd read our book, had applied the biblical principles we presented, and had found victory!

In this revised and updated edition of *Spiritual Housecleaning*, we share some of these stories with you. Why? To help you see even more clearly why living a life of purity and victory depends upon our forsaking things that dishonor Christ and His kingdom and to help you understand that evil has the same mode of operation wherever it exists around the world. Evil is neither creative nor complex. In fact, it's quite predictable.

So fasten your seatbelts. Some of the stories you will read will amaze you. But we aren't the least bit interested in your entertainment. Rather, we pray that you'll receive new revelation of the tactics of the enemy so that you can live free and set others free. Scripture clearly teaches that evil will become darker and righteousness brighter until our Lord comes for His Church (Isa. 60:1-3; Dan. 12:3; Matt. 13:24-43; 2 Tim. 3:13).

Let's prepare. The worst and the best are yet to come!

Eddie and Alice
Houston, Texas

❖

WHY WE WROTE THIS BOOK

Imagine there was a plague of snakes of biblical proportion in your city. The house in which you live became completely over-run with deadly, poisonous snakes. How important would it be for you to make sure *some* of the snakes were removed? You wouldn't even consider that an option, would you? Absolutely not! You would insist that *all* of the snakes be removed if you and your family were to continue living there. Could you sleep peacefully if you thought there might be *even one* poisonous snake left in your home? Hardly.

Would you believe there could be possessions inside your home right now that pose a spiritual threat to you and your family, just like poisonous snakes pose a physical threat? The average Christian family may not even be aware of the necessity to *spiritually clean* their house in order to experience the peace-ful presence of God.

That's why we wrote this book.

Many of us are suffering today because we have sometimes willfully, and sometimes ignorantly, invited possessions and behaviors into our homes that defile the atmosphere and give the devil the right to affect our lives and the lives of our children. This defilement can come in many forms: statues of foreign gods, "magic" charms, occult books, or perverse "souvenirs" of past sins. But whatever the form, God doesn't want us to possess defiled objects, for they invite the devil to wreak havoc with our hearts and homes. That is clearly not how Christ wants us to live. Paul tells us in 1 Corinthians 10:20, "I do not want you to have fellowship with demons."

To the uninitiated reader, some of what's contained in this book may sound a bit like superstition. We understand where you are coming from. Some might even conclude that our belief in a spirit world and faith in an unseen God is a superstition. But to us, superstition is placing faith in any person, place or thing other than the almighty God and His infallible Word. We unfold not legalism nor superstition but biblical principles and proven practices that can indeed free us, and our households, from any spiritual bondage.

That being said, Christ's cross and resurrection have established our authority over the devil. Since Jesus gives us His authority, we are to live on the offensive (Matt. 10:1; Luke 19:10; Eph. 6:10). For that reason, we should never fear the devil or demons. Jesus set the example for us when He taught us to pray, "Deliver us from evil" (Matt. 6:13, *KJV*). The Lord's deliverance is available to those who walk in the way of righteousness. With this knowledge, as children of the King, we exchange our fear for freedom. Yet to fully live in our inheritance, we must be sure there is nothing in our lives or in our homes that would hinder our fellowship with God.

What does purity of heart involve for us as Christians? What does it mean to love God with all our hearts, our souls and our minds? It means to not allow Satan access to any aspect of our lives, thereby keeping ourselves undefiled. It means that we don't give Satan any place or allow him any opportunity (Eph. 4:27).

Today is a new day for the Church! It's time for the Church of Jesus Christ to awaken from her slumber. We can no longer afford to wallow in the carnality of the world and expect the Lord to overlook it. Today, God is calling us to a new level of holiness. We need to cleanse the atmosphere of our homes as well as our hearts. This cleansing often involves the removal of certain physical possessions. But which ones?

We have written this book to teach you *how* to walk circumspectly and to exercise spiritual discernment (1 Cor. 2:15; Eph. 5:15). This may very well prove to be one of the most important books you will ever read, because its principles can provide the key to spiritual peace and security for you and your entire family.

We have a world to reach with the gospel! But before we can reach a fallen world, God must reach us. Our lives and our possessions should reflect God's kingdom rule. We're not to live under the tyranny of legalism or performance. We are to be godly and grateful because we know we owe everything to our Lord and Savior, Jesus Christ!

PART ONE

❖

SPIRITUAL HOUSECLEANING PRINCIPLES

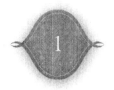

SPIRITUAL DISCERNMENT

The Indian sun blazed, raising temperatures to 118 degrees Fahrenheit by midday. People were dying due to the excessive heat. To protect themselves, most would work until about 10:00 A.M., retreat inside until sundown, and then resume their business and shopping.

Robert (our eldest son) and I (Eddie) were in Karapur, India, to teach at a Christian conference (and, by the grace of God, we managed to survive the heat!). More than 300 Indian Christians joined us there, bearing the intense heat as they rode bicycles, buses and trains—some for days—to attend the conference. Once there, they slept on concrete floors, bathed out of buckets and ate food cooked over outdoor fires.

We taught various subjects, but my teaching on spiritual housecleaning had the most far-reaching impact on this idol-worshiping culture. As I spoke about unbiblical heathen practices and cultural traditions, I could see my listeners removing from their bodies, their pockets and their purses the Hindu fetishes (i.e., string bracelets, necklaces and charms) they wore or carried in hopes that a particular god would protect or provide for them.

I gave the altar call. With zeal they brought those forbidden, spiritually defiled items to the altar and discarded them (Acts 19:18-19). Freedom rang out like church bells in the hearts of those precious people that day! Curses were broken, generational sin was severed and spiritual liberty was released. Some people were healed and others were saved. The next day we baptized 67 in a public city pond!

Robert and I left the hotel the day after our conference to catch our plane for the United States. We'd been gone from the hotel for about 30 minutes when we received a phone call telling us that the police had come to the hotel to arrest us—just minutes after we left. God spared us the trouble.

Why did they want to arrest us? Was it because 67 people had trusted Christ? Was it because 67 people had renounced their Hindu faith and been baptized? No. It was because we had taught them that their Hindu worship artifacts were evil, defiled and forbidden by God. The newspapers reported that we had offended and belittled their Hindu gods and that we'd converted 300 of their people. They didn't understand a thing about the true conversion of the 67 who'd received eternal life but instead focused on the 300 who disposed of their fetishes.

Wouldn't you agree that if our asking people to divest themselves of these things offended the Hindu priests so much that they sent police to arrest us, it's safe to assume that those things (or, rather, the Hindu "gods" behind them) held some sort of power over them? And for us to possess such things glorifies devils and grieves the one true God (Acts 24-29; 1 Cor. 10:18-22).

Genesis 35:1-5 gives us a biblical example of this truth:

And God said unto Jacob, "Arise, go up to Bethel and dwell there; and make there an altar unto God, who appeared unto thee when thou fleddest from the face of Esau thy brother." Then Jacob said unto his household and to all that were with him, *"Put away the strange gods that are among you,* and be clean and change your garments. And let us arise and go up to Bethel; and I will make there an altar unto God, who answered me in the day of my distress, and was with me in the way which I went." And they gave unto Jacob all the strange gods which were in their hand, and all their earrings which were in their ears; and Jacob hid them under the oak which was by Shechem. And they journeyed; *and the terror of God was upon the cities that were round about them, and they did not pursue after the sons of Jacob (KJ21,* emphasis added).

After Jacob and his family got rid of their objects of idolatry, God honored them. His presence went with them and put terror in the hearts of the people around them—people who might otherwise have attacked them. Today, the same power and favor of God is available to us, whether we are in India, America, Antarctica or anywhere else in the world! Time and again, for nearly 40 years, our experiences with spiritual housecleaning have shown this to be true.

Encounters with Demons

As itinerant evangelists in the 1970s, we traveled hundreds of thousands of miles, living in a motor home that we lovingly called our piece of "wheel estate." In fact, during that time we owned seven such vehicles before we stopped traveling! We conducted hundreds of evangelistic crusades in churches and football stadiums across America. We were blessed to see thousands of people come to Christ.

During those early years of our ministry, we did a great deal of personal counseling. Traveling as we did from town to town, we began to recognize spiritual patterns. Regardless of whether we were in a city, in suburbs or in small rural towns, we noticed similar things happening in the spiritual realm.

In the late '60s and early '70s, few books had been written about spiritual warfare or deliverance. *Pigs in the Parlor,* written by our friend the late Frank Hammond, was one of the first. Hollywood's burgeoning fascination with the demonic expressed itself in films like *Rosemary's Baby, Poltergeist* and *The Exorcist,* to name a few. Added to that was the massive influx of immigrants to the United States, who arrived with their family gods and religious cultural practices (many ready to build their temples and mosques right in our neighborhoods). Our land quickly became defiled. Don't misunderstand—America had her own demons. But our *Leave It to Beaver* days were over, and demonic manifestations exploded in this nation.

We encountered our first case of a demonized person in a large Baptist church in South Texas. Frankly, we were stunned to witness a "respected churchgoing woman" lying on the floor of her pastor's office, hissing and writhing like a snake, speaking with an unearthly male-sounding voice. From that moment, we were completely convinced that Satan was more than an evil idea or philosophy. He and his minions were real spiritual beings—like people without bodies—who had an intense desire to inhabit a human body to fulfill their lusts and desires and advance Satan's kingdom (Matt. 12:25-26,43-45).

Soon we were routinely counseling demonized people, leading them through deliverance from the demons that plagued them, many from birth. At the same time, we encountered people—godly people, believable people—who were experiencing poltergeists (mischievous demons who move objects), ghosts (demons masquerading as the deceased), and other troubling manifestations. Children were the most easily harassed by them. They suffered from insomnia, nightmares and more.[1]

As our experience grew, so did our understanding. We discovered that the demons that plagued people were in some cases strengthened by unholy possessions—defiled, forbidden objects that dishonored Christ (Deut. 7:25-26; Hos. 4:10-13; 1 Cor. 10:18-22). Almost weekly we saw people who, as they discarded those possessions, experienced freedom from demonic manifestations.

In Acts 19, we see how Ephesian believers destroyed their occult material when they saw the power of God at work through Paul. In that day, Ephesus was known as a witchcraft capital of the Roman world. It was a city famed for its written collections of occult spells, statues and images of the goddess Diana, and for the practitioners who used them. Paul shook the city up when he came preaching the name of Jesus in the power of the Holy Spirit. Through signs, wonders and deliverances, many believed. But it took a demonic attack on the seven sons of Sceva to show the Ephesian Christians that they needed to shut every door to evil activity in their lives (Acts 19:11-16). When this happened, those believers got the message: Jesus is the highest power in the universe! They then burned their books of the occult, rid themselves of idolatry, and confessed their sins publicly. What happened next? "The word of God grew mightily and prevailed!" (Acts 19:17-20).

Ministering Deliverance

One night in the '70s, during a revival meeting in a Southern state, there was a gathering at the pastor's home. One of the ladies in the group caught our attention. We both discerned a spiritual defilement about her. Jane (not her real name) was the music minister's wife, and her husband was out of town that week. Before the week was over, we found ourselves counseling with her concerning her sexual involvement with one of the teenage boys in the church. (Yes, she was sexually active with one of the church's own teens!)

We asked Jane about her salvation. This pretty young woman said she had been saved one night while driving her truck. A voice had whispered in her left ear, "Give me your life," and she had said, "Lord, I *do* give you my life."

"And to whom were you speaking?" we probed.

"What do you mean, 'to whom'?" she said. "I was speaking to God."

"How did you know it was God?"

"You mean it might have been a demonic spirit?"

She realized that from the moment she'd made that commitment, her life had begun a downhill slide. (If you ask God for a fish, He won't give you a serpent, but a devil certainly would.) In Matthew 7:17-20, Jesus said that the "fruits"—people's actions and character—show whether the source of that fruit is good and from God or bad and not from God. This woman's decision produced the bad fruit of growing oppression and uncontrollable sin in her life, which showed that she had unwittingly given her life to demons.

The bottom line? She was born again and delivered that week. All the issues came out for the necessary parties to bring correction.

Two weeks later, her husband called to tell us she was suffering from an overwhelming temptation to rekindle her sinful relationship with the boy. Through phone counseling, we discovered that she had a blouse and a necklace the young man had given her. Those gifts, we explained, were physical representations of their sin. They strengthened the "soul tie" (a spiritual attachment between people brought about through evil actions or unholy covenants between them). It wasn't until she destroyed them that she was set free. People can develop godly soul ties, like Jonathan and David (1 Sam. 18:1), or ungodly soul ties, like Samson and Delilah (Judg. 16:4-19).

Because we were traveling evangelists, we had far more experiences and encounters than we would have had were we pastors in one locale. One night in a tiny Tennessee church, we were in a pastor's study, trying to help Kim, a delinquent teenage girl. When Kim's unwed teenage mother conceived her, her mother and father (Kim's grandparents) out of shame tried to cover their daughter's sin. They sent her away until she gave birth to Kim. During that time, the family moved to another city and didn't tell extended family members about the pregnancy or the birth.

When Kim was born, her grandparents adopted her and never disclosed to her that she was actually their granddaughter, not their daughter. Kim was taught and believed that her birth mother was her older sister. One day, one of Kim's cousins discovered the deception and told her about it. Her parents (actually her grandparents) lied again and told her it was only a cruel prank. But she believed her cousin, and became depressed, suspicious and severely troubled. She didn't know who or what to believe.

Kim's mother and father (again, actually her grandparents) brought her to us for counseling. When they told us how they had lied to her, we insisted that they tell Kim the awful truth no matter how painful it would be. Kim could never build a healthy life on a foundation of lies and deceit. That night they disclosed to Kim that she was their granddaughter and that her "sister" was actually her mother. She was devastated, but in her heart she had known all along that something wasn't right. Kim had lived with a lie her entire life, and it affected her core identity.

For an hour we ministered deliverance to Kim without seeing the breakthrough we'd hoped for. We were stymied. It seemed we'd hit the proverbial brick wall. We prayed for God to reveal why we were so impotent against the spirits that bound her.

Then we noticed something in a lower bookshelf. The pastor's bottom bookshelf contained a copy of Anton Levy's *Satanic Bible* along with several other occult handbooks. We asked the pastor why he had them. He said he had bought them for research.

We explained to him that they were compromising the young lady's deliverance. We stopped our session, took the books outside to a trash-burning bin and set fire to them. It was almost impossible to get them lit, but after we did, the most amazing thing happened (since then we've seen this many times and hear about it often): No matter which side of the bin we chose to stand on, regardless of the direction of the slight breeze that night, the flames licked out at us. When we moved away from the bin, they licked farther, trying to reach us. It was almost as if the flames had minds of their own.

Once the books were destroyed, Kim was completely liberated by the Lord.

Spiritual Defilement in the Home

The woman's voice on the other end of the line sounded eerie and mystical. She had sought help from a Christian psychiatric hospital that had referred her to us. This divorced woman and her eight-year-old daughter lived alone, trapped in a world of darkness. The girl's father was a Unitarian pastor, but prior to that he had been an African witch doctor in a tribe known as the Leopard People. The now-abandoned single mom had extensive knowledge of the occult. And though she testified to having been recently born again, within the walls of her home, torment ruled.

At her request, we visited her home. Cats fearfully scurried from under our feet as our small prayer team approached the apartment door. When the woman opened the door, we were introduced to an atmosphere that almost took our breath away—it felt electric with evil.

Once inside, two large cats cowering near the refrigerator hissed at us, then disappeared within seconds. The electrical power flashed off and on until we commanded it to stop. To the right of the front door was a 10-foot bookcase filled with religious, heathen and occult books. She invited us to be seated and we began to discuss her problems.

She explained that her daughter was being harassed in the night by nightmares and apparitions. The child would awaken to see ghosts in her room. (The ghosts were actually demons appearing in the forms of an old African-aboriginal man and woman.) The concerned mother stated that at times the child would leap on top of the dressers and move about like a leopard. This precious little girl would sometimes wake in the morning with humanlike bite marks and claw scratches in the middle of her back.

One night, the frightened girl awakened her mother several times, complaining that flies were biting her. Each time her mother turned on the lights and searched the room but found nothing. The next morning when she opened the window shades, she found a mound of dead flies piled on her daughter's windowsill. This didn't surprise us—we know that Satan is sometimes spoken of as Beelzebub, the lord of the flies (Matt. 12:24-32; Mark 3:22).

The enemy had clearly been given authority to operate in their home. As we prayed and asked God for wisdom and discernment, we waited for the Holy Spirit's direction. At times the demonic reality was almost palpable. Spiritual impressions from the Lord (i.e., "the word of knowledge" [1 Cor. 12:8]) came to our team members as we cleansed the atmosphere with prayer.

All at once, as though the team had received the same revelation, we turned and stared at the wall of books—her huge occult library. We explained to the young mother that the books and the artwork acted as "bait" for the demons. (As flies are attracted to dung, demons are attracted to darkness.) Her library was an open invitation to demonic spirits and gave them legal right to defile her home and harass her and her child. These books, like a welcome mat, communicated to the unseen demonic world that they had the woman's permission to stay. Such items and artifacts may seem harmless, yet they hold significance to satanic spirits.

We urged the mother to discard the occult books. We even offered to dispose of them for her. She refused. She lamented over the money she'd invested in the books. We lovingly explained that the books symbolized contracts she'd made with the enemy, and that unless she forsook them, we'd have no authority over the demons that victimized them.

We begged for the sake of her daughter that she spiritually clean the house, but she turned a deaf ear to us. This woman's attachment to her occult library compromised her and her daughter's spiritual security and allowed the enemy to terrorize her child.

C. Peter Wagner shares an account of the power of idols in the ancient city of Athens. Sadly, we were unable to go any further.

The only place in the Bible where we find the phrase "given over to idols" (from the Greek *kateidolos*) is where Luke describes Athens in Acts 17:16. Athens was the idol capital of the ancient world, possibly comparable to Kyoto, Japan, today. The literature of that day describes Athens as a forest of idols in which it is easier to find a god than a human being. Certain streets had so many idols that pedestrian traffic was difficult. One observer estimated that Athens contained more idols than the rest of Greece combined!

Because idols themselves are only made of wood or stone or metal, some are not concerned about their presence. These idols, however, were not just any piece of wood or stone or metal. They had been carefully and intentionally crafted by human beings as forms in the visible world through which the forces of the invisible world of darkness were invited to control the lives of people, families and the city as a whole, locking the people in spiritual darkness. That's why we read that Paul's "spirit was provoked within him" (v. 16).[2]

Yet this is not the only illustration of defilement. Let's look at what happened to Joshua in the Old Testament.

A Piece of Cake?

"Now sir, let's not overreact," suggested Eliasaph, General Joshua's senior military adviser.[3] "We can relax now and give the men a break. Trust me—this one is going to be a piece of cake. According to our reconnaissance, there's no reason at all for you to send the entire Israeli army to attack such a small place as Ai. ["Ai" literally means "a heap of ruin."] I suggest that a reduced force of 2,000 or 3,000 troops will be sufficient to utterly destroy the city."

So the next morning Joshua sent 3,000 troops to annihilate little Ai. To their surprise, the feisty troops of Ai, ready for battle, killed 36 Israeli soldiers and chased the others from the gate of the city down the slope to the stone quarries. Israel's dispirited army was forced to retreat like a dog with its tail tucked between its legs.

Joshua was stunned when he heard the news. After all, the much larger city of Jericho, which they'd soundly defeated, still lay in smoldering ruins. *How could Eliasaph have so grossly underestimated the military capability of a small town like Ai?* Joshua wondered. *More important—where was God? And what about the promises He had made to them?* God had clearly said:

> Joshua, I am giving to you the land I promised Moses. I will always be with you and I will help you as I helped him. No one will ever be able to defeat you. So be strong and courageous! Do everything Moses taught you. Never stop reading the Book of the Law he gave you. Think about what it says day and night. Obey it completely and you will be able to take this land (Josh. 1:1-9).

Joshua called together an emergency council meeting of Israel's leaders. "Gentlemen," he said, "you will recall that Jehovah God promised us that He would never leave us and that we would never be defeated. Where do you suppose we went wrong when that handful of untrained, ragtag men disgraced our troops today? May I suggest, sirs, that we have a national emergency on our hands? And we must get to the bottom of this—*now!*"

So Joshua and the leaders tore their clothes and put dirt on their heads as a symbol of sorrow and repentance. They lay facedown on the ground in front of the Ark of the Covenant and cried out to God until sunset.

Then Joshua prayed:

> Lord, did you bring us across the Jordan just so the Amorites could annihilate us? If we had stayed on the

other side of the Jordan, none of this would have happened. Frankly, I'm speechless. It's shocking to realize that our army actually ran from our enemy today. Our people will soon think that You can no longer protect us. When our enemies hear of our humiliation, they are likely to become emboldened. They may even try to surround us and wipe us out.

The Lord answered Joshua:

General, get up off your face! I'm not taking prayer requests at this time. I told you that everything in Jericho belonged to me. What's more, I told you to destroy the city and everything in it. Instead, you and your people have stolen and hidden some of the booty for yourselves; and you've lied about it.

Because you've stolen stuff that was supposed to be destroyed, Israel itself has been set aside for destruction. I can't help you anymore until you do exactly what I've told you to do. And that's precisely why your army could not stand before the little band of men at Ai.

Tell the people that they'll never be able to stand against another enemy until they rid themselves of the abominable things that they've hidden. Tell them to prepare for worship. Tomorrow morning, when they gather for worship, I will identify for you the guilty tribe and point out the guilty clan and the guilty family. And I will show you the man who has stolen the forbidden things that have defiled Israel and have broken the sacred covenant I have made with you. That man, along with his wife, his sons and his daughters, must be executed by stoning. Their bodies and all of their possessions must be burned.

Early the next morning Joshua brought each tribe to the place of worship. There the Lord identified Judah as the guilty tribe and the clan of Zerah and Zabdi's family as the guilty clan and family. He showed them that Achan was the man responsible for violating Israel's contract with God.

General Joshua said, "Achan, is it true? Don't try to hide anything from me. Tell me what you've done."

"Yes, sir, it's true," Achan answered reluctantly. "I'm the one who sinned against the Lord God of Israel. While we were mopping up at Jericho, I found a beautiful Babylonian robe, 200 pieces of silver and a gold bar that weighed as much as 50 pieces of gold. *I wanted them for myself,* so I took and hid them in a hole beneath my tent."

So Joshua immediately sent men running to Achan's tent to retrieve the silver, the gold and the robe. They brought the defiled items back and laid them before the Lord so that Joshua and the rest of the Israelites could see them.

Then everyone took Achan, his sons and daughters, his cattle, donkeys, and sheep, his tent and everything that belonged to him, as well as the things he had stolen, to a nearby valley.

Once there, Joshua said, "Achan, you've caused us a lot of trouble. Now you are in trouble."

The people of Israel stoned Achan, his family and his animals to death. They built a fire and burned the bodies, along with all the possessions and the cursed things that Achan had stolen. They covered the ashes with a big pile of rocks. And that place is still known as Achor—Trouble Valley.

Then God stopped being angry with Israel and gave them the city of Ai (Josh. 8:1).

Ten Lessons We Learn from This Story

I. God's Promises to Us Are Awesome!

Our great God is a promise-keeper. He has given us thousands of promises in His Word. Salvation is only the beginning of God's promises. Beyond our salvation experience there are countless treasures waiting for us to experience in Christ, because God "has blessed us with every spiritual blessing in the heavenly places in Christ" (Eph. 1:3). Furthermore:

> We have everything we need to live a life that pleases God. It was all given to us by God's own power, when we learned that he had invited us to share in his wonderful goodness. God made great and marvelous promises, so that his nature would become part of us. Then we could escape our evil desires and the corrupt influences of this world (2 Pet. 1:3-4, *CEV*).

Have you realized that once you are born again, His nature becomes part of you?

2. God's Promises Are Often Contingent on Our Obedience

In order for us to enjoy the benefits that God has promised, we must trust Him and believe that He keeps His Word. Our faith activates His promises in our lives. However, many of God's promises are conditional. They are contingent upon our obedience. We call them God's if/then promises.

With regard to our salvation, He's promised that "if" we believe in our hearts and "if" we confess with our mouths, we shall be saved (Rom. 10:9).

With regard to His forgiveness of our sins, God has promised that "If we confess our sins, He is faithful and just to forgive us our sins and to cleanse us from all unrighteousness" (1 John 1:9).

God had made covenant with Joshua and had given him promises too. He promised to give him the land He had promised Moses (Josh. 1:1-4,15); to be with him and to help him, as He had helped Moses (Josh. 1:9); that he would never be defeated (Josh. 1:5).

But with those three promises, there were three commands, or conditions: be strong and courageous (Josh. 1:6); do everything Moses taught (Josh. 1:7); read, meditate on and obey the Book of the Law (Josh. 1:8).

Achan had failed to do everything God had asked of him. He had taken that which God had forbidden the Israelites to take—things that God had designated for destruction—and had hidden them in a hole in the ground beneath his tent. Although the Lord doesn't suggest that a demonic power was attached to the Babylonian garment, the 200 pieces of silver or the 50 gold shekels, He had said that those things were accursed and should be avoided. Why would God want the Israelites to avoid them—unless they brought evil with them? Certainly Achan's act of disobedience had opened the door to darkness.

Consequently, the main idea of this story is that to disobey God brings a curse, for disobedience is inherent in idolatry, which is the worship of demons (Deut. 32:16-18).

3. Physical Things Sometimes Carry Spiritual Significance

Throughout Scripture we see evidence that physical things can carry spiritual significance: the lamb's blood that God had the children of Israel apply to their doorposts (Exod. 12:7-13); the Tabernacle, its furnishings and utensils (Exod. 26–27); water baptism (Luke 3:21-22); the Last Supper (Matt. 26:28; 1 Cor. 11:23-25); miraculous handkerchiefs and aprons (Acts 19:11-12); healing oil (Jas. 5:14). But perhaps the clearest example is found in the Old Testament and is one we're all familiar with—Moses' brass serpent:

> And the people spoke against God and against Moses: "Why have you brought us up out of Egypt to die in the wilderness? For there is no food and no water, and our soul loathes this worthless bread." So the Lord sent fiery serpents among the people, and they bit the people; and many of the people of Israel died. Therefore the people came to Moses, and said, "We have sinned, for we have spoken against the Lord and against you; pray to the Lord that He take away the serpents from us." So Moses prayed for the people. Then the Lord said to Moses, "Make a fiery serpent, and set it on a pole; and it shall be that everyone who is bitten, when he looks at it, shall live." So Moses made a bronze serpent, and put it upon a pole; and so it was, if a serpent had bitten anyone, when he looked at the bronze serpent, he lived (Num. 21:5-9).

The brass serpent that God instructed Moses to elevate on a pole for the children of Israel to see offered a solution for their sin. True, it was only a brass serpent on a pole—an inanimate object; yet it provided healing power to those who were bitten by the poisonous snakes. If they looked upon the brass serpent, they were healed. Today we understand even more about the significance of that brass snake. The serpent that Moses lifted up was actually a symbol of Christ who, when lifted upon the cross, became sin for us. Our sin was judged in Him and He died in our place. In dying, as they looked upon the brass serpent and were saved from their sin and received physical life, so we look to Jesus' atoning sacrifice upon the cross to be saved from our sin and receive eternal life (John 3:14).

Nine hundred years later, when King Hezekiah was cleansing the Temple, "He removed the high places and broke the sacred pillars, cut down the wooden image [Asherah] and *broke in pieces the bronze serpent which Moses had made; for until those days the children of Israel burned incense to it*" (2 Kings 18:4, emphasis added).

Amazingly, after all those years, an object that God had originally designed for Israel's healing had become a god they worshiped! So, He called it defiled.

Physical things can have a divine or even a demonic significance. We experienced this firsthand at the 1996 International Conference on Prayer and Spiritual Warfare in Charlotte, North Carolina. After teaching at the conference, we were looking for a room where we could do individual counseling. As we opened the door to a small room backstage, we saw pieces of dog feces laid out in the shape of a cross on the floor in the center of the room, pointed toward the pulpit in the adjoining room. We felt a witch had placed them there to curse the meetings. Witches believe that physical items provide points of contact for demonic spirits. So their use of fetishes is a common ploy for deception and control.[4]

This is no time for us to be flaky or superstitious, but it is time to learn how to walk circumspectly with spiritual discernment. Some of the things in this book may appear to you as mere superstition. According to our culture's definition of "superstition," some might conclude that even our belief in a spirit realm and our faith in an unseen God is a superstition. As we've said, to us, superstition is placing faith in any person, place or thing other than the almighty God and His infallible Word. The spiritual dimension is real. It preceded the physical dimension. The Apostle Paul said, "So we fix our eyes not on what is seen, but on what is unseen. For what is seen is temporary, but what is unseen is eternal" (2 Cor. 4:18, *NIV*).

4. God Forbids Us to Possess Certain Things

It's inappropriate for God's children to possess certain things. When He saved us, He didn't patch up our old lives; God made us new creations! Paul wrote, "Therefore, if anyone is in Christ, he is a new creation; old things have passed away; behold, all things have become new" (2 Cor. 5:17). Because of our new life in Christ, God expects from us new living as well. We are to put off the old and put on the new. Ephesians 5:8-11 says:

> For you were once darkness, but now you are light in the Lord. Walk as children of light (for the fruit of the [light] is in all *goodness, righteousness,* and *truth*), finding

out what is acceptable to the Lord. And have no fellowship with the fruitless works of darkness, but rather expose them (emphasis added).

In Exodus 20:3, God forbade the children of Israel to have
any other gods. He is a jealous God—jealous of our trust (Deut.
4:24; 5:9). In Deuteronomy 18:9-13, God warned them not to
engage in witchcraft and astrology. He explained that such activities are abominable to Him:

> When thou art come into the land which the Lord thy
> God giveth thee, thou shalt not learn to do after the
> abominations of those nations. There shall not be
> found among you any one that maketh his son or his
> daughter to pass through the fire, or that useth divina-
> tion, or an observer of times, or an enchanter, or a
> witch, or a charmer, or a consulter with familiar spirits,
> or a wizard, or a necromancer. For all that do these
> things are an abomination unto the Lord: and because
> of these abominations the Lord thy God doth drive
> them out from before thee. Thou shalt be perfect with
> the Lord thy God (*KJV*).

In the Old Testament we see lists of things that dishonor
God and should not be found among His people. These things
suggest that there are other gods, which violates the first four
commandments.

> Take careful heed to yourselves, for you saw no form
> when the Lord spoke to you at Horeb out of the midst

of the fire, lest you act corruptly and make for yourselves a carved image in the form of any figure: the likeness of male or female, the likeness of any animal that is on the earth or the likeness of any winged bird that flies in the air, the likeness of anything that creeps on the ground or the likeness of any fish that is in the water beneath the earth. And take heed, lest you lift your eyes to heaven, and when you see the sun, the moon, and the stars, all the host of heaven, you feel driven to worship them and serve them, which the Lord your God has given to all the peoples under the whole heaven as a heritage. Take heed to yourselves, lest you forget the covenant of the Lord your God which He made with you, and make for yourselves a carved image in the form of anything which the Lord your God has forbidden you. For the Lord your God is a consuming fire, a jealous God (Deut. 4:15-19,23-24).

This list is still valid. The Father is grieved if we possess statues of other gods—or any objects that connect us to a spiritual source other than the one true God. Such items as graven images of other gods (Exod. 20) are strictly forbidden, because they open the door to supernatural deception, turn people away from God and hinder people's spiritual and physical health.

5. The Use of an Item Can Establish Its Spiritual Significance

Most objects are neither good nor evil in and of themselves. However, the way that we use them can establish their spiritual significance.

One day we wandered into a shop in Madras, India. We were souvenir shopping before leaving to go to the airport. There on an elevated platform sat an artisan holding a log with his bare feet as he skillfully carved it with hammer and chisel.

"What are you making?" Eddie asked the man.

"I'm carving a god," he replied.

"And which god are you carving?"

"I'm carving Ganesh, our god of prosperity," he answered.

To his amazement, Eddie aggressively lurched toward him and shouted, "Hurry! Finish it! Quickly. . . quickly!"

"Why? What's the rush?" the man asked.

Still animated, Eddie said, "Sir, look out the windows of your shop. Your streets and sidewalks are littered with lepers and beggars. Your people are malnourished. Many are starving. Finish your 'god of prosperity' and get him into the streets so he can do what he's supposed to do!"

We'll never forget the expression on the man's face. It seemed to say, "You know, what you just said makes a lot of sense." (And perhaps he had an additional awareness that none of his other idols had ever worked either.)

There certainly was nothing intrinsically wrong with the log the man was carving. Yet when carved into an object of heathen worship, though it provided no solution to poverty, its spiritual significance was contrary to the kingdom of God (Deut. 4:15-19, 23-24). Indeed, decades of experience with deliverance ministry has convinced us that demons sometimes attach themselves to certain persons, places and things.

Referring to man-made idols, Paul said, "We know that *an idol is nothing* in the world, and that there is no other God but one" (1 Cor. 8:4, emphasis added). So in and of themselves idols are simply powerless objects, and the meat sacrificed to them is nothing more than meat.

However, Paul went on to explain, "What am I saying then? That an idol is anything, or what is offered to idols is anything? Rather, that the things which the Gentiles sacrifice they sacrifice to demons and not to God, and I do not want you to have fellowship with demons." (Deut. 32:17; 1 Cor. 10:19-20).

Since the beginning, people have used inanimate handcrafted objects to commune with demons. The spiritual strength behind the idol is demonic. The demons use the idol to receive worship from people who are deceived and desperate enough to worship them. When they worship, pray to, or honor idols, people are worshiping demons. As a result, the idols they worship can become tools of the devil; and even their own lives are then open to demonic influence. Demons lead deceived people astray directly or indirectly through the mediation of these objects.

You might ask why Paul had no problem eating meat that had been offered to idols. His only reluctance to do so was that he wouldn't offend a weaker brother (1 Cor. 8:3-13). Wouldn't the meat, which is a physical object, be subject to a demonic attachment as well?

Of course we can't know for certain. But perhaps food is a special case, since it's created by God to satisfy a universal need. To the contrary, objects that have only one purpose—to operate outside of the governance of God and to actively and independently work against Him—call for either deliverance or destruction.

A good example of such an instance relates to the day a cable movie channel mysteriously appeared on our television. We called the cable company and said, "Ma'am, we are receiving HBO on our television and we didn't order it."

"That's okay," the lady answered politely.

"No, it's not okay," we insisted. "Let us speak to your general manager."

The general manager came to the phone and said, "Folks, I was told about your call. Don't you worry; we're not going to charge you for the HBO."

"You're not going to charge us?!" we responded hotly. "Sir, you had better hope that we don't charge you! We don't let the city of Houston dump their garbage in our front yard, and we're not about to allow you to dump your 'garbage' in our living room!"

It's amazing how fast that movie channel disappeared!

6. Illicit Possessions Can Separate Us from God's Purposes, Protection and Power

God's protection of us and His power released through us are directly related to His purposes for us. When we willfully—or ignorantly for that matter—step away from God's purposes for our lives, we step out from under His protective care.

You can clearly see this in the life of Samson. He forsook God's call on his life to live the life of a fool. Then one day Delilah awoke him: "And she said, 'The Philistines are upon you, Samson!' So he awoke from his sleep, and said, 'I will go out as before, at other times, and shake myself free!' But he did not know that *the LORD had departed from him*" (Judg. 16:20, emphasis added).

It's not that God refused to protect Samson. Samson, in his recklessness, forsook God's purpose; and when he did, Samson ceded God's protection and power. Do you agree? Do you see how deception in our lives keeps us from God's wonderful plan for our future?

7. One Person's Crime Can Result in Corporate Consequences

We learn an amazing lesson in this case of Joshua and the nation of Israel (Josh. 7). Only one person—Achan—had sinned; yet God held the entire nation accountable! Look at these plural references in what God said to Joshua:

- *Israel* (the whole nation) committed a trespass (Josh. 7:1).
- The anger of the Lord was kindled against *the children of Israel* (all of them) (v. 1).
- *Israel* sinned (Josh. 7:11).
- *Israel* transgressed God's covenant (v. 11).
- *Israel* took the accursed things (v. 11).
- *Israel* stole (v. 11).
- *Israel* put the stolen items among their own things (v. 11).
- Therefore *the children of Israel* could not stand before their enemies (Josh. 7:12).
- *They* turned *their* backs before *their* enemies, because *they were accursed* (v. 12).
- Neither would God be with *them* anymore, unless they destroyed the accursed from among *them* (v. 12).

Incredibly, one man's sin brought repercussions upon the entire nation. Achan's sin produced corporate consequences. As a result, 36 soldiers (husbands, sons and fathers) needlessly died in the first futile battle against Ai. As a consequence of Achan's sin, an entire nation was left defenseless and fearful. And, in some ways, this is the saddest of all: Achan's family—his wife, his sons and daughters, who as far as we know were innocent—were executed along with him.

We also see corporate guilt, as well as redemption, as a New Testament principle. In Romans 5:19, we read, "For as by one man's disobedience many were made sinners, so also by one Man's obedience many will be made righteous."

This corporate nature of the Christian life is somewhat foreign to us as Americans—we typically pride ourselves on our independence. We have yet to learn that as members of Christ's Body we weren't designed by God to be independent, but rather to be interdependent upon each other. And as Paul wrote, "If one part of our body hurts, we hurt all over" (1 Cor. 12:26, *CEV*).

So, if you are a Christian man with pornography hidden in your home or a Christian lady who's addicted to soap operas and romance novels, you're very likely contributing to the spiritual impotence of Christ's Church.

8. When We Seek God, He Will Reveal the Defiled Things

How can we know which of our possessions dishonor the Lord? Thankfully, we don't have to guess about these things. God has given us His Spirit. Jesus promised, "However, when He, the Spirit of truth, has come, He will guide you into all truth" (John 16:13). When we pursue purity and ask the Father, He will show us if any of our possessions are displeasing to Him. The truth is, God reveals to heal!

We experienced just such a healing after God revealed the unseen demonic intruder who at times invaded our peaceful home. We loved our home nestled in the woods far from the busy traffic and hurried lifestyles of Houston, our nation's fourth largest city; but an evil presence (and sometimes odor) would appear in a particular corner of our large family room. We could sense it, and our children often complained when sitting in that part of the room.

One evening, as we were pacing the room in prayer for special church services that were to begin later that night, I (Alice) sensed that evil presence again. Enough was enough! I sought the Lord as to why. Unwilling to wait any longer, I closely checked all the trinkets and magazines near the corner of the room. When I examined the fireplace mantle, my gaze settled on a beautifully bound, six-volume set of books. I'd inherited the elegant collection from a deceased aunt. Neither Eddie or I had ever opened them—they simply were ornaments to grace our mantle. Inside the books were pages filled with lithographs of ghosts, gargoyles and graveyards with spirits ascending from the tombstones. The author wrote of depression, death and fear. I was appalled! After I repented to the Lord for allowing these books into our home, I spoke aloud and broke all contracts with demons that used the books as an access point into our home. I trashed the books and the problem never recurred.

Thankfully, because Christ died in our place, unlike Achan and his family who died for having the accursed things, you and I will not be executed. Hallelujah! But as the believers in Acts 19 did, we need to rid ourselves of anything that defiles our lives and our homes. We'll talk more (in chapter 4) about what those things might be.

9. We Should Ruthlessly Rid Ourselves of Wicked Things

Self-indulgent Achan had abused God's grace and presumed upon God's promises. The result was a welcomed victory to the Canaanites. But as a consequence of their unexpected loss, Israel was awakened, reformed and reconciled to God.

Scripture tells us, "Now these things [Old Testament accounts] became our examples, to the intent that we should not lust after evil things as they also lusted" (1 Cor. 10:6). Having read this experience of Joshua and the children of Israel, we shouldn't have to be forced to allow God to inspect our hearts and our possessions.

In the New Testament we read about a revival in the city of Ephesus:

> Many who had believed came confessing and telling their deeds. Also, many of those who had practiced magic brought their books together and burned them in the sight of all. And they counted up the value of them, and it totaled fifty thousand pieces of silver. So the word of the Lord grew mightily and prevailed (Acts 19:18-20).

Our friend C. Peter Wagner states that the value of the occult items the Ephesians destroyed that day was approximately 5 million U.S. dollars!

God is about the work of His kingdom. And "the kingdom of God is not meat and drink; but righteousness, and peace, and joy in the Holy Ghost" (Rom. 14:17, *KJV*). Our possessions should express the righteousness, peace and joy of God's kingdom. If they don't, the moment the Lord reveals spiritual contamination to us, we should repent and unrelentingly rid ourselves of it for Christ's sake.

Such a vigilant course of action may seem unnecessary—but perhaps you can learn something from Jim, a new believer who had left behind a life of sin and now was passionate about Jesus, his new Lord! When Jim heard the teaching of spiritual housecleaning, he remembered that his Rolex watch had been a gift from a woman with whom he had lived in adultery. Jim desired to please the Lord, so early the next morning he drove to the city lake, stepped out of his Cadillac, removed the gold and diamond-encrusted watch and threw it as far as he could into the murky water. Later that day he told us about his experience.

"Why did you throw the watch away?" we asked him.

"Because it was symbolic of the unholy relationship I experienced with that woman," he replied.

The watch was more than a watch. To Jim it represented an evil contract that sealed the covenant of sin he had with the woman. However, the watch wasn't inherently evil. It wasn't a golden dragon or designed as a snarling serpent. It was only a very expensive gold watch. Although Jim could have prayed over it, repented for the sin it represented, broken the contracts that it symbolized and sanctified it to the Lord, he opted to destroy it. Had he asked for our counsel, in that case we would have encouraged him to sell the watch and invest the money in the kingdom of God as a gift to his church or to the poor. Let wisdom prevail!

But the point is this: Never underestimate the wiles of the devil—he will explore every option and examine every possible entry way to your life!

10. Obedience Restores Our Fellowship with God and Reinstates His Purposes

Unauthorized possessions hinder, and in some cases prevent us from being blessed and used of God. As it was with Joshua and the children of Israel, personal cleansing will restore God's presence, reinstate His protection and re-ignite His power in our lives. (Read in Joshua 8 how the Lord delivered the city of Ai into the hands of the children of Israel.)

Prayer Assignment

Father, in the precious name of Jesus, I am so blessed that You love me enough to show me the truth about my life, my home, my children and possessions. Lord, I don't want to be like Achan who kept a thing that You called defiled. Would You right now, holy God, reveal to me anything with which I need to deal? I desire holiness, and You are holy; so show me the un-holy actions in my life or the unholy possessions in my care or the unholy covenants I have made.
In Jesus' name I pray. Amen.

Notes

1. To learn more about deliverance, see Alice Smith, *Delivering the Captives* (Grand Rapids, MI: Bethany House, 2006), available at www.prayerbookstore.com
2. C. Peter Wagner, *Confronting the Powers* (Ventura, CA: Regal Books, 1996), pp. 204-205.
3. The following is a loose adaptation of Joshua 7; General Elisiaph is a character created for the sake of readability.
4. A fetish is an object witches use to vex the environment with magic powers; an amulet is a charm to ward off disease or evil spells.

WHO WANTS TO LIVE IN A HAUNTED HOTEL?

Have you noticed that more and more television shows involve the supernatural? Still, Americans assume haunted houses to be things out of Hollywood movies and Stephen King novels. Others attribute them to an overactive imagination. As a preteen, I (Eddie) remember how my older cousin Bill turned off the lights to tell us about the haunted house on the hill above his parents' home. Of course, he waited until dark to tell the story, but he never persuaded me to go with him to check it out!

Today Alice and I firmly believe in haunted houses, haunted church buildings—even haunted hotels!

One evening in 1990, we received a call from the chief of security at one of Houston's major hotels. The chief, a retired 20-year police veteran, told us this amazing story.

"Two weeks ago a Haitian voodoo organization, comprised of more than 100 men and women dressed in white, held a conference in our hotel. They rented several rooms at the hotel and used our main ballroom to conduct their ceremonies. Though we thought it a bit bizarre, they stationed their own security guards at the entrances of the ballroom. These huge men refused to allow anyone, including my officers and me, near the proceedings.

"One of my security officers inadvertently ventured into the ballroom one night through one of the dining room service doors. He found the room pitch dark except for candle-light. In the midst of the room sat a man chained in a chair. The worshipers were in a trance, and a bloody ceremony was taking place. The security officer said that it so frightened him that he slammed the door, ran downstairs, jumped into his car and drove home.

"Since then," the chief continued, "our hotel has experienced major problems. We have had an abnormal number of thefts from the rooms, arguments and even fistfights among the employees, inexplicable car accidents in front of the hotel and workers calling in sick in record numbers. The hotel organization is in shambles. Furthermore, all of the employees—including me—are afraid to enter the ballroom where the voodoo ceremonies took place."

He continued, "Tonight, as I drove home from work, around the 610 Loop and out Highway 290, I was so fearful that I would have an accident I drove 15 miles per hour on the shoulder of the road. When I arrived home, my wife suggested that I exercise to relieve my stress. As I jogged my normal neighborhood route, every time a car came up behind me, I grimaced and my body tensed. In my imagination I could almost feel a bullet sear its way through my body. I just knew I was about to be shot. I've called because someone told my wife that you might be able to help me."

"How long does it take to get to the hotel?" Eddie asked.

"Thirty minutes," he replied.

"Great, we'll meet you there in 30 minutes."

Upon arrival at the hotel, we met the nervous security chief in the lobby and the three of us took the elevator to the fifth floor where the main ballroom was located. As we walked over to the entrance to the ballroom, the security chief stood stiffly to the left of the elevator doors, unwilling to move an inch. From a distance, he threw the keys to us. We opened the door and stepped into the dark cavernous room.

The light switches, we discovered, were on the back wall at least 100 feet away. We walked to the center of the long, dark room. The atmosphere was oppressive, as if a million angry, invisible hornets were swarming around us. The air felt electric as waves of spiritual energy pushed past and swept over us. The enemy was desperately trying to frighten us away.

Quietly yet confidently we began to pray. As Nehemiah repented on behalf of others (Neh. 1:6), we repented to God for what had happened in that room just days before; we asked God to remove the defilement. Then, with authority, Eddie told the evil spirits to leave. Suddenly, as if the tide of spiritual darkness rolled out, the demons departed, and soon the room felt pure and clean. Even the security chief felt safe enough to enter the ballroom.

A week later he called to thank us. He said, "The thefts, the fights, the accidents and the illnesses are gone. Inexplicably the morning after you prayed through the ballroom, a Bible study was spontaneously formed in the employee lounge!"

Spiritual Atmosphere

Today increasing numbers of Christians are taking a second look at the spiritual environment in their homes. They want their homes, as well as their lives, to reflect the presence of Christ, but this is not often their experience.

As we have searched to find the reasons why, we have noticed three things that contribute to the atmosphere in a home: the attitudes and behavior of the family members who live there; the possessions stored there; and the predominant spiritual presence.

Attitudes and Behavior

Through our attitudes and behavior, intended or not, we invite either an evil presence or the Holy Spirit's presence into our homes. Bad attitudes and behavior on the part of those with authority (usually parents) have an adverse effect on the atmosphere of the home and on all who live there. We need only look to an example from nature to see how parents set the tone for home life:

> The first month of a nightingale's life determines its fate. I had always thought that a nightingale's incomparable song was instinctive and inherited. But it is not so.
>
> Nightingales, to be used as pets, are taken as fledglings from nests of wild birds in the spring. As soon as they lose their fear and accept food, a "master bird" is borrowed that daily sings its lovely song, and the infant bird listens for a period of about a month. This is the way the master bird trains the little wild bird.

If it has a good teacher, the infant bird will learn from experience to produce as beautiful tones as its teacher. But if an infant bird is brought to such a teacher after being raised by wild nightingales, there is always failure, as long experience has shown.

The illustration of the nightingales reminds me that many children's problems could be solved if they just had parents who were "good singers"—parents who take responsibility for the mood or emotional tone of the home—parents who understand that their children are absorbing the emotional atmosphere and learning to respond to life as their moms and dads did.[1]

We are each responsible for our own sin and its effect upon our spouses and our children. Why blame the devil for what we choose to do? When we blow it, we should repent—repentance keeps us close to the Lord and prevents the devil from gaining a foothold in our lives.

Is it easy to keep a positive spiritual atmosphere in the home? Of course not. It requires us to pursue peace, live in humility and harmony and resist the temptation to repay evil with evil, insult with insult, but instead to respond with blessing. (1 Pet. 3:8-9; 11)

When anger rules a person's life, spirits of anger, hate, malice, resentment, bitterness, jealousy, rage and the like are drawn to that person like ants to a picnic.

When love, joy and peace rule a person's life, demons are repelled and God is blessed. The Holy Spirit is at home in the presence of these Kingdom attributes. It's true. He inhabits the praise of His people (Ps. 22:3)!

Our Possessions

As bad attitudes and behavior can adversely affect the spiritual atmosphere of our homes, so can our possessions. What do we mean?

If we were to warn you that to leave certain things around your house would attract rats, would you leave those things lying around? Of course you wouldn't! Yet unholy things among our possessions both dishonor God and attract demons.

In the Old Testament God warned His people to tear down the Asherah poles, dismantle heathen altars and destroy idols (Judg. 6:25-26). They were to have nothing among their possessions that dishonored God. As mentioned, the newly saved Ephesians were led to burn their books that related to the gods and goddesses of their former religions (Acts 19:19).

When we consider these passages, let's remember that our possessions reflect our priorities. They testify of our true spiritual condition. Never did this truth hit home more convincingly than while we traveled as itinerant evangelists.

Once, while shopping for a new travel trailer, we went to see one that belonged to a couple who, like us, were ministers. We were impressed with their trailer—it was exactly what we were looking for.

They insisted that we spend all the time necessary to examine it. As we measured the miniature closets to see if our stuff would fit, we opened a large drawer under one of the twin beds. To our shock and disappointment, it was filled with pornography. As you might imagine, in a flash this couple's "spiritual stock" (in our eyes) plummeted. Hell certainly smiled to see their porn-filled drawer, and we were sickened.

People like these rarely realize that such putrid possessions invite the enemy to make himself at home. Once demons infiltrate a home, they set out to harass, to influence and to manipulate family members to more illicit levels of behavior. The spiritual atmosphere of the home gradually shifts as the cycle continues unabated. The Holy Spirit, grieved, withdraws as He did from Samson's life (Judg. 16:20). And, as Christians, although we are in Christ, we move out of the place of God's blessing. Even worse, —we become spiritually vulnerable and a potential embarrassment to the Lord Jesus.

No doubt God's angels wring their hands. And God, who wants to bless and protect us, sadly watches as we squander our opportunities. In our ignorance and in some cases our willful disobedience, we forfeit the Father's blessings and His angelic assistance and the enemy celebrates.

The Predominant Spiritual Presence

The spirit world is real—it coexists with the natural world. Both angels and demons share your home from time to time with you and your family. Jesus said the Holy Spirit is like a wind that comes and goes (John 3:8); Satan is described as a roaring lion that walks about the earth (1 Pet. 5:8). The ratio between the two, which is in constant flux, is one ingredient that establishes the spiritual atmosphere of your home, though most of us can't see that dimension. Spirits that belong to these opposing kingdoms—Satan's kingdom of darkness and God's kingdom of light—coexist with what we see physically.

We do not look at the things which are seen, but at the things which are not seen. For the things which are

55

seen are temporary, but the things which are not seen are eternal (2 Cor. 4:18).

Babies and small children naturally see the spiritual dimension. They see angels and demons. It's likely, when a child reports that there is a monster in his or her room and the parents shine a flashlight in the closet and under the bed to prove the child is mistaken, it's the parent, not the child, who needs instruction. Let us relate a story from our family life that convinced us that young people see the spirit realm.

●When our youngest son, Bryan, was about 14 years old, he came into the kitchen one morning for breakfast. He said, "Dad, the strangest thing happened to me last night as I was about to fall asleep. I looked up into the darkness of my room and against the ceiling hundreds of demons sneered, scowled and snarled at me."

"What did you do, son?" I asked.

"I did what you and Mom taught me to do. I told God how tired I was and asked if He would get rid of them."

"What did God say?" I pressed him.

"He said, 'No,' Dad."

"Did He tell you why?"

"Yes. He said, 'Bryan, I want you to let them watch you sleep.'"

Wow! Can you imagine how humiliated that team of demons must have been, whose only assignment was to scare a young servant of the Lord instead to see him peacefully fall asleep amid their threats?

I said, "Bryan, go and get your Bible." When he returned with his Bible I said, "Read Psalm 3 to me." He read:

LORD, how they have increased who trouble me! Many are they who rise up against me. Many are they who say of me, "There is no help for him in God." But *You, O LORD, are a shield for me,* my glory and the One who lifts up my head. I cried to the LORD with my voice, and He heard me from His holy hill. *I lay down and slept; I awoke, for the LORD sustained me. I will not be afraid of ten thousands of people who have set themselves against me all around.* Arise, O Lord; save me, O my God! For You have struck all my enemies on the cheekbone; You have broken the teeth of the ungodly. Salvation belongs to the LORD. Your blessing is upon Your people (emphasis added).

"Bryan," I explained, "The Lord just let you experience Psalm 3!"

Gift of Discerning Spirits

There is also a spiritual gift the apostle Paul mentions as "discerning of spirits" (1 Cor. 12:10). This gift, demonstrated in various ways, includes a person's capacity to see or to sense the spirit realm more clearly than most.

One expression of this gift is the ability to actually see spirit beings. This shouldn't come as a surprise. After all, Scripture is filled with examples of people who saw angels. A classic example involves the prophet Elisha and his servant, who awoke only to discover they were surrounded by an army on horses and chariots. The servant became anxious. He feared for his life. Elisha told him, "Don't be afraid. . . . There are more troops on our side than on theirs" (2 Kings 6:16, *CEV*).

Then Elisha prayed saying, "Lord, I pray, open [my servant's] eyes that he may see" (2 Kings 6:17). And the Lord opened the young man's spiritual eyes and, to his complete surprise, he saw the entire mountain covered with an angelic host on horses and fiery chariots, ready to defend them!

Good and Evil Spirits

Who are the angelic host? And who are the demons that they wage war against? Angels are God's spiritual helpers He's used from the beginning to minister on Earth. (Heb. 1:14) Amazingly, there are 99 references to angels in the New Testament alone! Some examples include:

- Two angels appeared in Sodom (Gen. 19).
- God's angels met Jacob (Gen. 32).
- Angels appeared to Moses (Exod. 3).
- David interacted with an angel (1 Chron. 21:16).
- An angel appeared to Mary to announce the birth of Jesus (Luke 1).
- An angel appeared in a dream to Joseph (Matt. 1).
- An angel ministered to Peter (Acts 12).

Demons, counterparts to God's angels, are evil spirits subject to Satan. Many believe that these dark spirits are the fallen angels of whom the Bible speaks—those angels that rebelled with Lucifer in heaven, and were expelled and cast onto the earth (Isa. 14:12-15; Luke 10:18). However, there are other plausible speculations as to what demons might actually be.

Demons, like Satan, wander the earth. Some spirits aimlessly wander through buildings; others may be specifically assigned to them. Some pretend to be ghosts or spirits of the departed dead. Why do they do this? They do it because they desperately seek to interact with people. Satan still seeks whom he may devour (Luke 11:24; 1 Pet. 5:8).

We also know from experience that demons crave a material presence. They continually search for a physical object made of wood or stone or a human or animal body that they can manipulate for their purposes.

Spiritual Houseguests

Why would we assume the ministry of angels would be less today than in biblical times? According to the end-time prophecies of Jesus and references in the book of Revelation, angels are very active in the last days—and of course in heaven for eternity!

Prayer Assignment

Lord, You are my deliverer and King. Thank You for the Word of God that says in 1 John 4:4, "You are of God, little children, and have overcome them, because He who is in you is greater than he who is in the world." With this authority that comes from Your living in me, Lord Jesus, I ask that You replace any demonic influence in my home right now with Your abiding peace. Reveal to me anything about my attitudes or behaviors that would be attractive to the enemy. [List each issue the Lord brings to mind.] I repent for my attitude toward . . .

_____

_____

_____

_____

Now Lord, please show me anything among my belongings
that dishonors You, whether in my home, car or business.
[List each belonging.] I will destroy it to please You in every
area of my life. Thank You for showing me the way.
In Jesus' name I pray. Amen.

Note

1. Sinichi Suzuki, quoted in Valerie Bell, *Getting Out of Your Kids' Faces and Into Their Hearts* (Grand Rapids, MI: Zondervan Publishing, 1994), pp. 76-77.

SYMPTOMS OF SPIRITUAL POLLUTION

We stood on the spot where their church once was. Their shattered building, washed off its foundations by the raging floodwater, now floated eerily down the San Jacinto River.

The pastor told us of the problems his congregation had encountered with their building, including the escrow account, the unexplainable putrid odors and the odd behavior of certain people in the church.

"What could've caused all of this?" the pastor asked.

"It sounds to us like your land is defiled," I (Alice) answered.

"It's strange you'd say that. Did you know that the movie *Grave Secrets,* starring Sally Field, was made about this neighborhood? The developers didn't tell the new residents that their homes were built atop what was once a Native American burial ground. After the residents moved in, many of them began to smell strange odors, see their light bulbs burst for no apparent reason and experience increased sickness. Some of them filed lawsuits against the developers, while others simply abandoned their houses. I'd hoped that we were located far enough away from the site of the actual burial ground to not be affected by it."

The Symptoms

The Old Testament speaks of defiled land more than 15 times. The Hebrew word translated "defiled" is *taw-may*, which means foul or contaminated, especially in a ceremonial or moral sense. Homes as well as land can be defiled or spiritually polluted.

In Numbers 25:1-13, we read how the Israelites committed whoredom when they sacrificed and worshiped the god of Moab, Baal of Peor. The defilement so permeated the entire tribe that one Israelite brought a Midianite prostitute into the tabernacle where Moses and the congregation had gathered to worship.

When Phinehas the priest, also the grandson of Aaron the high priest, saw this, he killed both the man and the prostitute with a javelin. As famed radio commentator, the late Paul Harvey would say, "And now . . . the rest of the story." When the abomination ended, the plague against the Israelites stopped; but not before it had killed 24,000 people (Num. 25:8-9).

Do you see it? Their ongoing illnesses and the deaths of 24,000 people were the result of spiritual defilement. What a tragedy! Since spiritual pollution is one of the causes of sickness, we'd do well to conduct a spiritual inventory of our homes.

Symptoms that could signal sources of defilement:

- Sudden chronic illness; continual nausea and headaches
- Recurrent bad dreams and nightmares
- Insomnia or unusual sleepiness

- Behavioral problems; restless, disturbed children
- Relational problems—continual fighting, arguing and misinterpreted communication; general lack of peace
- Bondage to sin
- Ghosts or demonic apparitions (to which young children are particularly susceptible)
- Poltergeists (the movement of physical objects by demons)
- Foul, unexplainable odors
- Atmospheric heaviness, making it hard to breathe

As cleansing the atmosphere for the Israelites stopped their problem, so also cleansing the atmosphere of our homes often solves these problems.

What Constitutes Defilement?

We've been privileged to help Christians discard thousands of dollars worth of personal possessions that God revealed to them had polluted their homes. These were things that didn't reflect the goodness, righteousness, truth and character of God. We have thrown out furniture, clothing, jewelry, paintings, occult items, sculptures, statues, movies, books, magazines, music, posters, CDs, DVDs, games, religious icons and even rosary beads. What could possibly be wrong with rosary beads? Before going any further, please open your heart and mind. We have many wonderful born-again Catholic friends to whom God is revealing truth as well. Here is what we've noticed.

As with any man-made item that assists people with prayer, the rosary—or similar items traditionally thought of as aids to prayer—are also used in idolatrous worship.

Ralph Woodrow, in his book *Babylon Mystery Religion*, writes:

The Catholic Encyclopedia says, "In almost all countries, then, we meet with something in the nature of prayer-counters or rosary-beads." It goes on to cite a number of examples, including a sculpture of ancient Nineveh, mentioned by Layard, of two winged females praying before a sacred tree, each holding a rosary. For centuries, among the Mohammedans (Muslims), a bead-string consisting of 33, 66, or 99 beads has been used for counting the names of Allah. Marco Polo, in the thirteenth century, was surprised to find the King of Malabar using a rosary of precious stones to count his prayers. St. Francis Xavier and his companions were equally astonished to see that rosaries were universally familiar to the Buddhists of Japan. Among the Phoenicians a circle of beads resembling a rosary was used in the worship of Astarte, the mother goddess, about 800 B.C.[1]

If you are from a Catholic background, prayerfully consider the following experience:

As we ministered in the beautiful and historic northeast European nation of Latvia we drew large crowds. However, for some reason, the ministry anointing was hindered.

One night, as I (Eddie) struggled to fall asleep, I cried out to the Lord, "Why, Lord? Why is it so difficult here?" I heard no answer. Soon I was fast asleep.

At approximately 3:00 A.M. I awoke suddenly from a deep sleep. I felt compelled to find a pen and paper. It was clear that the Father wanted to speak with me. For the next 20 minutes I wrote down what I heard Him say: "The spiritual restriction you are experiencing is a result of religious icons—specifically the crucifix."

I knew the cross and the crucifix are different images. The cross is empty—Jesus isn't there. The crucifix, on the other hand, isn't empty. It's a cross with a dead Jesus still hanging on it. But why would the crucifix be a problem? I felt the Holy Spirit say, "The crucifix, in Satan's mind, is a 'photograph' of his finest hour. He succeeded in killing Jesus. Whether carved in wood, chiseled in stone, painted in oils or molded in bronze, a crucifix presents to the world a dead, helpless God, which provokes many to pity but few to saving faith."

Then I remembered all of the nations we'd visited. How often we'd seen Catholic paintings, icons and images of Jesus, most of which historically present Him as weak, emaciated, sickly or dead—incapable of helping either Himself or others.

What of Mary, His mother? She's typically depicted as vivacious, attractive and in the pink of health. She's either holding baby Jesus or, to the contrary, holding His dead body—though Scripture never suggests that she actually did.

We are certainly grateful for Christ's sacrifice on the cross. He died in our stead. Through His death we have salvation from our sins. But the cross isn't to be displayed as a tragedy. To the contrary, it was a mighty victory!

The Holy Spirit continued, "The Crucifixion is not the highpoint of the gospel. The empty cross and the open tomb are! Go back and reread the sermons in the New Testament." I did. Sure enough, the apostles preached, "Jesus of Nazareth . . .

you have taken by lawless hands, have crucified and put to death. This Jesus God has raised up, of which we are all witnesses" (Acts 2:23-24). (We urge you to stop now and read Acts 2:23-36; 3:15; 4:10; 5:30-31; 10:39-41; 13:28-37; 17:30-32.)

It is true! The gospel message that the apostles preached, and for which they died, contains three times as much about His resurrection as it does His crucifixion! The cross and the tomb are both empty! We are to declare to the world, "Jesus is alive!"

Then the Holy Spirit reminded me of our visit to Jordan. In the plane was a photo of the king of Jordan. On the wall of the airport in Ammon, Jordan, was a larger-than-life photo of the king of Jordan. His picture was in our cab. As we drove through the streets, we saw his picture on billboards and painted on buildings. It was in our hotel lobby. The Lord reminded me that an image constantly kept before the people reinforces the message.

God reminded me of what the apostle Paul wrote in 1 Corinthians 15:13-14:

> But if there is no resurrection of the dead, then is Christ not risen. And if Christ is not risen, then our preaching is empty and your faith is also empty.

My heart broke to realize that nations that have elevated and embraced the crucifix, with its dead, helpless Jesus, have been the hardest to reach with the gospel of Christ. Thankfully, millions of people worldwide are receiving the revelation of this truth—the power of the gospel is in the risen Savior (Rom. 10:9-10; 13)!

The next night, we returned to the conference venue and shared with the people the message we'd received from the Lord.

They were struck with the revelation. Joyfully and expectantly, they removed their necklaces and bracelets that contained the crucifix. As they did, all heaven broke loose. Some were born again, others were delivered. Some people shouted, while others danced in victory. One striking breakthrough was the salvation and deliverance of a white witch.

We've learned through the years that it's one thing to *give things* to God that we might live for Him, but it's another thing entirely, as the rich young ruler learned, to *give up things* for God that we might die to this world and escape its hold on us.

When you consider your possessions, don't forget religious paraphernalia! Perhaps your undue attachment to religious images actually hinders rather than helps your Christian walk. If you struggle with this, just remember:

> However, when He, the Spirit of truth, has come, He will guide you into all truth; for He will not speak on His own authority, but whatever He hears He will speak; and He will tell you things to come (John 16:13).

Loving Housecleaning

Remember, we don't conduct spiritual housecleaning out of fear, superstition or legalism, but out of wise and loving devotion to God. Our children need to see their parents as fearless examples to follow. They need to see the sufficiency of Christ in us. Our goal should be to have homes that honor Christ, homes in which He is comfortable and in which the Holy Spirit's presence is predominant.

We're not called to live life in a vacuum. We were born on a battlefield. Although Christ soundly defeated Satan by His death on the cross (Col. 2:15), God has left the enemy here so we might learn to overcome. God has promised to set His table before us "in the presence of [our] enemies" (Ps. 23:5). So fear not, brothers and sisters—Christ is our fortress and our shield and He will honor our efforts to keep a godly house. As we walk in obedience to Him, He assigns His angels to minister to us! Hebrews 1:14 says, "Are they not all ministering spirits sent forth to minister for those who will inherit salvation?"

Prayer Assignment

Father, Your Word is a light unto my path. Light my path right now, as You reveal any spiritual pollution from my family or from previous residents that is present here in my home. I repent for my ignorance and that of my forefathers (Neh. 1:4-11). Wash me from these offenses with Your blood, Lord Jesus, and grant me complete freedom and victory. In Jesus' name I pray. Amen.

These are the items I am going to discard. (Make a list.)

_____

_____

_____

_____

_____

_____

_____

These are the items I am going to sell. (Make a list.)

_____

_____

_____

_____

_____

_____

_____

The money I receive from the sale of these items will go to: _____.

Now, because we should not close our eyes when we address the enemy, with your eyes open, declare with the authority of Christ:

> *In the powerful name of Jesus, I break any and all*
> *unholy contracts, agreements or alliances I have made with*
> *the kingdom of darkness and I command you, demons,*
> *to leave my home, my family and me—now!*

Next, get up and find these items and place them in a trash bin or carefully burn them in a safe place. If an item is valuable and is not intrinsically evil—that is, it has unfavorable meaning only to you—sell it or give it away. *Be free!*

Note

1. Ralph Woodrow, *Babylon Mystery Religion* (Riverside, CA: Ralph Woodrow Evangelistic Association, Inc., 1966), p. 27, quoting *The Catholic Encyclopedia*, vol. 15, pp. 459 and 484.

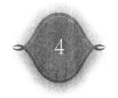

CAUSES OF
SPIRITUAL
POLLUTION

Before God called me (Alice) into the ministry, I was a real estate agent in northwest Houston. I had one listing that puzzled me—it was an attractive home in an upper-middle-class neighborhood and was newly painted inside and out, with updated decor and new carpet. Potential buyers seemed impressed with the house and constantly expressed an interest. Yet for some reason, it simply wouldn't sell.

The young Christian couple seeking to sell the home was equally confused and disappointed. After I prayed with them about the sale, we decided to have a team of intercessors pray through the property. As our prayer team drove up to the vacant house, our youngest son, Bryan, said, "Mom, I believe the Lord just showed me that there are satanic symbols painted on both the inside walls of the garage and on the ceiling of this house."

Since I had been through the house countless times and would have certainly noticed those things had they been there,

I politely thanked him and told him I didn't think that was the case! He must have been mistaken.

However, when we walked in, out of respect to my son, I mentioned to the owners what he had told me. They looked at each other in shock. The wife explained, "The last renters of this house spray painted satanic symbols on the walls of the garage. As you know, we have repainted, but come with me, and I'll show you a bit of the design that can still be seen behind the hot water heater." Sure enough, just as she said, we could still see the partial outline of a pentagram. But where were the symbols on the ceiling? The ceiling hadn't been re-painted and there were no satanic symbols visible.

Then Eddie remarked, "Wait a minute. There are two ceilings in this house. The one we see and the ceiling in the attic space that we can't see." We located the attic stairway, climbed in with our flashlight, and to our amazement there was a large black pentagram spray-painted on the ceiling in the attic space.

We led the owners to repent to God on behalf of the renters who had defiled their home. (This is called "identifi-cational repentance." It's not that we're guilty of their sin. It's like an apology to God on behalf of another who's sinned. You'll find Nehemiah's example in Nehemiah 1:6-7.)

Next, we walked through the house, anointed it with oil and dedicated it to the Lord. As we drove away, we sensed in our hearts that God had heard us and that the curse had been lifted. Sure enough, after being on the market for more than six months, their home sold for full price fewer than 12 hours later!

A Demonic Visitation Versus a Demonic Habitation

If you engage in intercession and effective spiritual ministry, you'll likely encounter demonic spirits from time to time. Jesus certainly did when He walked the earth. Like Jesus, we'll never have the luxury of living in a demon-free zone. To the contrary, we are in a real spiritual war and Satan is not shooting blanks. It is serious business to be serious about Christ and His kingdom! But there is a difference between a demonic *habitation* and a demonic *visitation*.

The house we mentioned earlier had become a *habitation* of demons. In such cases, demons are assigned to, or have simply decided to dwell in, certain locations. In this case demonic spirits had been attracted there by the sin of the previous renters.

Such a *habitation* is quite different from the *visitation* often encountered by those who serve God. Fact is, if you plan to serve God on the front lines of Kingdom warfare, prepare to occasionally confront the enemy. They *will* visit you from time to time. Trust us, we know!

One night after a very intense deliverance of a young woman, we were awakened to what sounded like golf-ball-size hail beating on our roof. Yet we were totally shocked when we looked out the window. There was no rain, hail or even the slightest breeze. But the demonic visitation was still present. We weren't going to let the enemy intimidate us—we commanded the angry demons to shut up and leave us alone. The noise stopped and we fell asleep.

When we obey the Holy Spirit, He is pleased to manifest His peaceful presence. When we obey evil spirits they are pleased to manifest their impure presence. This has to do with legal ties or contract rights we give them (Rom. 6:16).

Has the devil ever intimidated you? If so, what did you do about it?

Aimless or Assigned?

A pastor friend of ours explained a night visitation in which a demon tried to strangle him in his sleep. We've experienced this before, so we understood his alarm. We said, "Pastor, can't you just imagine the poor demon who drew the lot to take on the assignment of strangling you? We're sure he begged and pleaded not to go, but his boss sent him anyway." We're convinced that in many cases it's more painful for demons than it is for us! For this pastor is a fearless, anointed man of God.

However, a demonic visitation is not the same as a demonic habitation. When demons inhabit a place, just as when they inhabit a person, it will require the ministry of deliverance to evict them. In a real sense, deliverance for a dwelling is much like deliverance for a person. One identifies the offenses that were committed, destroys the contracts made with darkness, removes the things that seal or symbolize the contract and enable darkness, and then dedicates one's home to God.

Sources of Defilement

Sources of spiritual defilement can take any shape. Below is a list—some of these items are instruments of the darkness; others can become instruments of darkness as a result of our unhealthy attachment to them. (This list is representative, not comprehensive.)

- Things related to heathen worship (voodoo dolls, spirit masks, snakes, dragons, thunderbirds, phoenixes, etc.)
- Things that are related to past sin (necklace, ring, love letters, photos)
- Things with unknown history, which are not inherently evil by design (Pray about the item. Dedicate it to the Lord. If the problem persists, then discard it.)
- Things that have become gods in our lives (collections, antiques, clothing, money, jewelry, etc.)
- Ouija board (also known as a witch's board)
- Games like *Dungeons and Dragons, Masters of the Universe, Pokemon*™ (a Japanese word meaning "pocket monster") and certain video games with witchcraft references, extreme violence, demonic or occult entities and images, or sexual perversion
- Buddhist, Hindu or other Eastern worship artifacts
- Certain indigenous art or pagan worship items, Egyptian ankh (the cross with a loop on top)
- Items related to Satanism, witchcraft, New Age, yoga, Unity, zodiac, crescent moon, crystal ball, pyramids (ancient obelisks or the Asherah poles of the Old Testament) and the martial arts
- Things related to astrology, horoscopes and geomancy, Edgar Cayce, Jean Dixon
- Comic books, rock posters, hard rock music and materials with obvious images of darkness
- Pornography of any kind (including explicit sexual videos, books, magazines, cable and satellite TV, the Internet and any media yet to be developed)

- Art with obvious demonic representations such as snakes, spirits, death, gargoyles, skulls, dragons, etc.
- Material related to Mormonism, Jehovah's Witnesses, Unity Church, Scientology, ancestral worship, Islam, Rosicrucianism, Zen, Hare Krishna, etc.
- Things relating to secret societies like Freemasonry, Eastern Star, Knights of Malta, Skull and Bones, etc.
- Certain children's books or movies, such as *Harry Potter* books or Disney's *The Sorcerer's Apprentice*, that encourage children to seek spiritual power unauthorized by God (specifically when the hero or heroine identifies with witchcraft and when the occult is presented as normal or, worse, preferable)
- Good-luck charms, amulets, fetishes
- Masonic aprons, books or rings, oriental ying and yang symbols, fortunetelling with tea leaves, Tarot Cards, talisman, etc.
- Movies with occult messages, extreme violence, excessive foul language or explicit sexual content
- Books (novels that focus on sensuality or death and destruction)

Perhaps you think that some of the above-mentioned items are harmless—even fun. But dealings with the devil aren't harmless. We always pay a price.

Never was it clearer to us than during a series of revival services in a southern Texas church some years ago. A lady and her daughter walked down the aisle and tearfully shared with us how they had consulted an Ouija board the night before:

We sat on either side of the board and followed the instructions. We asked, "What is your name?" The pointer, haltingly at first, then very directly, spelled "Death." Then we asked it, "Where are you from?" The pointer spelled "Satan." Fear filled our hearts. Terrified, we asked, "How far does your power reach?" The board then spelled, "To the blood."

In case you have further doubts regarding the seriousness of something like a Ouija board, listen to God's warning in Deuteronomy 18:9-14:

When thou art come into the land which the LORD thy God giveth thee, thou shalt not learn to do after the abominations of those nations. There shall not be found among you any one that maketh his son or his daughter to pass through the fire, or that useth divination, or an observer of times, or an enchanter, or a witch, or a charmer, or a consulter with familiar spirits, or a wizard, or a necromancer. *For all that do these things are an abomination unto the* LORD *and because of these abominations* the LORD thy God doth drive them out from before thee. Thou shalt be perfect with the LORD thy God. For these nations, which thou shalt possess, hearkened unto observers of times, and unto diviners: but as for thee, the LORD thy God hath not suffered thee so to do (*KJV*, emphasis added).

Heathen Souvenirs

A retired missionary couple sought our help with their rebellious, drug-addicted teenage son. We were appalled upon visiting their home to find their entire house decorated with heathen worship artifacts they had brought back as souvenirs from the foreign mission field where they had served. They thought that their home was a display of cultural curios, when in fact their souvenirs were nothing less than glorified images of demonic gods! They never guessed that their home was a satanic shrine! Can you imagine how that grieved the Holy Spirit? Is God bringing to mind anything like this in your home?

One instance that comes to my mind involved a family that I (Alice) led to Christ. A ghost continually troubled their two preschool sons. Our investigation revealed a large painting in their living room. This beautiful Southwest Indian painting seemed harmless at first. The painting depicted the body of a fallen Indian brave being burned on his funeral pyre. Above the flames the brave's "spirit man," astride his "spirit horse," ascended into paradise.

The label on the back of the painting explained that the artist was a shaman, who came from a long lineage of shamans. It further explained that this particular artist assigned a spirit being to each of the paintings he produced. Sure enough, when the painting was removed (without the knowledge of the small boys), the ghost (demonic spirit) was never seen again.[1]

God is very clear when He reveals the things in our lives that will bring blessings or curses. For example, He states, "Cursed be the man that maketh any graven or molten image, an abomination unto the Lord, the work of the hands of the craftsman, and putteth it in a secret place" (Deut. 27:15, *KJV*).

Even Stephen King?

One family who had a problem with spiritual entities roaming through their house at night invited us to pray through their home. The Lord revealed several unholy things as we prayed through each room. We were about to leave when we asked, "What's in the attic?"

"Nothing," the father replied. "We don't keep things in our attic."

"Yes, you do," we persisted. "The Lord just told us that one of your problems is in the attic. How do we get up there?"

The husband led us into the garage and placed a ladder under the opening. When we crawled into the attic we discovered a large cardboard box filled with Stephen King novels. The owners were shocked. Previous owners had left them there. That night we removed and destroyed the books and the supernatural manifestations ended.

You never know where you might find defilement. Keep an open mind—Satan is clever; he'll use any available means to separate you from God's will for your life.

Halloween

This chapter wouldn't be complete without touching on the issue of Halloween. Now keep in mind that years ago, when we were new parents, we too dressed our kids in costumes and take them door to door in our immediate neighborhood to trick-or-treat. We were sensitive enough to the Lord not to dress them as witches, skeletons, monsters or other evil personages. Since we did this for the enjoyment of our children, we didn't feel we were engaged in anything ungodly.

However, light (revelation) is given where light is received. In His time, God revealed to us that Halloween is inherently evil. This is because although Halloween is a religious day, it is not a Christian day. The origin of Halloween is the Celtic festival of Samhain, lord of death and evil spirits. Long before Christ (over 2,000 years ago), Druids in Britain, Ireland, Scotland, France, Germany and other Celtic countries observed the end of summer by making sacrifices to Samhain. The Celts considered November 1 as "the day of death" because the leaves were falling. They believed that Muck Olla, their sun god, was losing strength and Samhain, lord of death, was overpowering him. Further, they believed that on October 31, Samhain assembled the spirits of all who had died during the previous year.

Druid priests would lead the people in diabolical worship ceremonies in which horses, cats, black sheep, oxen, human beings and other offerings were rounded up, stuffed into wicker cages and burned to death. This was done to appease Samhain and keep spirits from harming them, for it was believed at this time that all of the wandering spirits would get hungry. If you set out a treat for them, they would not trick or curse you. Hence we have the origin of trick or treat. Tom Sanuinet, former high priest of Wicca, had this to say about Halloween:

> Trick or treat is a reenactment of the Druidic practices. The candy has replaced the human sacrifices of old, but it is still an appeasement of those deceptive evil spirits. The traditional response to those who do not treat is to have a trick played on them. Giving Halloween candy is

symbolic of a sacrifice to false gods. You are participating in idolatry.[2]

When we saw the spiritual implications of Halloween, we decided that the celebration doesn't please or glorify the Lord. So, rather than celebrate Halloween, we celebrated our children every October 31. We turned off our porch light (a signal to others that we weren't participants in the festivities), took our children to their favorite restaurant, and then to their favorite entertainment. To end the evening, we took them to the candy aisle of the local grocery and allowed them to fill a bag with the candy of their choice. They were thrilled! As parents, we didn't prevent them from enjoying the evening. We celebrated them without worry about razor blades or needles in their candy. (Yes, we governed their consumption of the candy.)

Today, many churches offer Halloween alternatives including carnivals, harvest festivals, prayer vigils and glory gatherings where there are no references to Halloween. Instead, wholesome games are played, Christian songs are performed and Christian videos shown. Others use Halloween as a night to pass out gospel literature. Whatever you choose to do, "Do not be overcome by evil, but overcome evil with good" (Rom. 12:21).

One More Night with the Frogs

Now that we've examined where those cobwebs might be found in your spiritual house, let's talk about just how clean you want your house to be. Most people want their homes to be spotless; isn't that what we want for our souls as well?

Not everyone wants to be so thoroughly cleansed. When we meet such folk, we are reminded of Moses and Pharaoh, and are intrigued by Pharaoh's answer to Moses with regard to the plague of frogs in Egypt. You may recall that God sent a plague of frogs and the Egyptian magicians added to it. Interestingly, in their attempt to "compete" with God, they only compounded Pharaoh's problem! The Egyptians had frogs in their bread and frogs in their beds—they were overrun by frogs!

> Then Pharaoh called for Moses and Aaron, and said, "Entreat the LORD that He may take away the frogs from me and from my people; and I will let the people go, that they may sacrifice to the LORD." And Moses said to Pharoah, *"Accept the honor of saying when I shall intercede for you, for your servants, and for your people, to destroy the frogs from you and your houses, that they may remain in the river only."* So [the pharoah] said, *"Tomorrow."* And [Moses replied], "Let it be according to your word, that you may know that there is no one like the LORD our God" (Exod. 8:8-10, emphasis added).

Pharaoh's palace was littered with frogs; yet when Moses asked him, "When do you want me to rid you of these frogs?" Pharaoh replied, "Tomorrow." *Tomorrow?! What's wrong with right now?!* Why would anyone want to spend one more night with the frogs?!

Are you content with one more night with the frogs? Some Christians are willing to live lives that are *almost* plague free. Free enough to get to church once a week. Free enough to live a moral life, have a good job and food on the table, but not free enough to really impact the kingdom of darkness and advance the kingdom of God.

Living in the Spirit

You might wonder what steps you can take to avoid encounters with darkness. The answers are all in God's Word. Read it; study it. Keep God's most important commands close to your heart. We are commanded to walk in the light if we're to fellowship with Christ (1 John 1:7).

> And have no fellowship with the unfruitful works of darkness (Eph. 5:11).

> But you are a chosen generation, a royal priesthood, a holy nation, His own special people, that you may proclaim the praises of Him who called you out of darkness into His marvelous light (1 Pet. 2:9).

> The night is far spent, the day is at hand. Therefore let us cast off the works of darkness, and let us put on the armor of light (Rom. 13:12).

> Do not quench the Spirit. Abstain from every form of evil (1 Thess. 5:19, 22).

> Do not give the devil a foothold (Eph. 4:27, *NIV*).

Prayer Assignment

Lord Jesus, I am so sorry for my involvement in the occult, and that of my children, which I thought was harmless. Now I realize it was not harmless. I see it and I repent in Your presence. Please cleanse me from my sin and free me from the devil's torment.

Make a list of books, artwork and items that God is speaking to you about removing.

_____

_____

_____

_____

_____

_____

_____

_____

_____

_____

*(With eyes open) I command any spirit of witchcraft or
antichrist spirit to leave me now. You have no right to my life.
In the powerful name of Jesus, I command you to leave my
home, my family, my possessions and me!*

Notes
1. Art from most cultures is based on religious or spiritual images and influences. A classic example is the use of the dragon in Chinese art. The dragon is one of the Bible's descriptions of Satan. Western art, for the most part, is based on natural images and influences (e.g., seascapes, landscapes, portraits). When it comes to artwork, we should exercise caution and discernment. Much Native American art has no spiritual implications whatsoever. I (Eddie) am part Cherokee, so I'm not criticizing any people group.
2. Christian Youth Alliance, Long Beach Island Student Center, Ship Bottom, New Jersey, email: cya@computer.net.

WHERE YOU NEVER THOUGHT TO LOOK

Years ago, a woman who suffered from bondage and sickness for many years asked us to send a team to pray through her house. As I (Eddie) walked past her desk the Lord gave me an impression.

"I believe this lower drawer contains something unholy," I said. She opened the drawer and pulled out a shoebox filled with old love letters from a former inmate in the state penitentiary. Her voice cracked with emotion and her eyes filled with tears as she explained that she'd been his pen pal.

The prisoner wrote passionately of his deep love for this lonely, vulnerable lady. He even proposed marriage, though he had no true romantic intentions. He cultivated the phony relationship so that he could list her among his references to procure his early release from prison. When he was later released, he failed to appear. Not only had he lied to her, but she never laid eyes on him! It was all a cruel hoax—he had used her.

"Why do you keep these letters that are filled with lies?" I asked.

She tearfully admitted, "Sometimes on lonely nights I pull out this box, curl up by the fire and read them, trying to re-feel my faded dreams."

I explained that she had allowed a stronghold of lies to be built in her mind. The letters were symbolic of the enemy's successful campaign. After some counsel, she became angry at the deception and renounced the contracts she'd made with the lying spirits.

It's time for us, the Church, to get angry over what Satan does! Too many of us feel that anger is sin. Not necessarily! Scripture says, "Be ye angry, and sin not" (Eph. 4:26, *KJV*). Paul urges us to "abhor [intensely hate or loathe] that which is evil" (Rom. 12:9, *KJV*). This woman's freedom and inner healing came when she burned the letters.

Unholy Soul Ties

She had been diagnosed as having 127 personalities, M.P.D. or "Multiple Personality Disorder" (see glossary). As we ministered to her, we noticed that she wore a strange pendant. We asked who'd given it to her. She explained that she and her best friend had exchanged pendants.

"Your friend has the same diagnosis as you, doesn't she?" we inquired.

She nodded yes. Sure enough, her friend was also hospitalized with multiple personality disorder. Both women were demonized and bound together in an unholy alliance (glossary). The necklaces were symbols of their union. She couldn't be set free until she renounced the unholy soul tie and destroyed the necklace (it was a symbol).

After our team of ladies ministered to her for three days she went home free—with only one joyful, Christ-filled personality!

We've worked with people who've suffered from depression and related symptoms. Many of them experienced freedom when they destroyed their spiritual journals or diaries in which they had recorded their negative, depressing thoughts. They had documented the enemy's success by writing down their "stinking thinking," and gave the devil a foothold as they logged their complaints against God, declaring—even documenting—His "failure" and the devil's success in their lives!

The lady with M.P.D. mentioned above had been counseled to record her thoughts and feelings. To be free, she had to discard a large boxful of negatively written ramblings and emotional rants against God that covered a period of more than five years! What an insult they must have been to the Father.

The example above is what we call an unholy soul tie. Such ties are often symbolized by gifts that include: souvenirs, trinkets, books, stuffed animals, photos, music albums, jewelry, love letters, clothing, furniture and wall hangings.

Remove old love letters; rid yourself of jewelry, pictures and clothing that represent and encourage emotional, physical, psychological or spiritual attachment; break free from your past and walk in the newness of God (Eph. 5:8, *AMP*).

Many who had believed came confessing and telling their deeds. Also, many of those who had practiced magic brought their books together and burned them in the sight of all. And they counted up the value of them, and it totaled fifty thousand pieces of silver [a piece of silver was about a day's wage]. *So the word of the Lord grew mightily and prevailed* (Acts 19:18-20, emphasis added).

Is it possible that our failure as Christ's Church to purify our homes and our lives keeps God's Word from prevailing mightily? Absolutely!

Throughout history, when people have made covenants and contracts with each other, they've sealed them with gifts (1 Sam. 18:3-4). So, it's important that we not only break the contracts, but also rid ourselves of any gifts that symbolize and seal the contracts we've made. Do you have any "souvenirs of sin"? Have you cleaned your closets, cabinets, dresser, attic or basement lately?

> And what agreement hath the temple of God with idols? For *ye are the temple of the living God*; as God hath said, I will dwell in them, and walk in them; and I will be their God, and they shall be my people. *Wherefore come out from among them, and be ye separate, saith the Lord, and touch not the unclean thing; and I will receive you,* And will be a Father unto you, and ye shall be my sons and daughters, saith the Lord Almighty. Having therefore these promises, dearly beloved, let us cleanse ourselves from all filthiness of the flesh and spirit, perfecting holiness in the fear of God (2 Cor. 6:16–7:1, *KJV*, emphasis added).

Possessions with an Unknown Past

Some items in our homes have an unknown past. They may be things that we've inherited, found by chance or purchased at a garage sale.

When we were newly wed and lived on a more modest income, we would tease that our home was decorated in early pawnshop. Actually, early garage sale would have been a bit closer to the truth!

Now let's be realistic—not superstitious. Let's say that you have an antique family heirloom about which you know little or nothing. Should you discard it? Read on.

Scripture records at least three occasions when God instructed His people to take, for their personal use, things that had been previously owned by unholy people.

1. When Israel defeated Jericho (Josh. 6:24)
2. When Israel defeated Ai (Josh. 8:27)
3. And in Egypt, the children of Israel were told upon their departure to borrow the jewels, silver, gold and clothing from the Egyptians for their journey (Exod. 12:35-36).

At least in these three cases they weren't concerned about any defilement from these items. Why? It was because God had given them the okay.

If an item has an unknown history with no obvious evil overtones, then exercise wise judgment. If you have a spiritual uneasiness about it, pray and sanctify it to the Lord. For that matter, all of your possessions should be given to God! Afterward, if there's still a question, remove that particular item from your house temporarily. Put it in your garage. (It should go without saying, don't ask anyone else to keep it at his or her house.) Look for any evidence that it was the cause of your problems. If so, get rid of it. If, after you remove the object, the same restlessness is present in the home, then the problem may lie in another area. So, keep up the search until you find the culprit. Remember, no material possession is worth more than the sweet, peaceful presence and protection of the Holy Spirit!

Sins of the Previous Owners

A young family from our church needed my (Eddie's) help. Neither of their two young sons had ever peacefully slept in the baby's room, which was located next to the master bedroom. When their second son was born, they moved their oldest son across the house to a third bedroom, where he soundly slept for the first time in three years. What then was the problem in the baby's room?

Our son Bryan and I dropped in one night to pray. We went through the baby's room with a fine-tooth comb. There was no object that was representative of evil. From the wallpaper to the toys, it seemed the perfect room in which a baby could rest.

Then the Lord showed Bryan three evil spirits standing in the center of the room. "Son, describe them to me," I said. He did. One appeared as an old woman, another as an old man—but "One," he said, "is huge, Dad!"

"Well, let's start with the big one," I said dryly. At that, he burst out laughing.

"What's so funny?" I asked.

"Dad," he replied, "you should have seen the look on his face when he heard you say, 'Let's start with the big one.'"

We cleansed the nursery and blessed it. Undoubtedly these three spirits had disturbed the babies' sleep. But I wondered what had given them a right to be in the home of this loving Christian family?

We'd found and corrected the problem, but as we turned to leave, something unusual caught my eye. There was a screen door eye screwed into the door jam *outside* of the bedroom door, and a corresponding hole on the bedroom door where there had once been a screen door hook. I reasoned that such a restraint wouldn't have been needed to keep a pet locked in the room. One would simply close the door. Nor would the eye and hook restrain an adult. It must have been placed there to keep a child in the room.

When we arrived home, I mentioned our find to Alice. She told me, "Eddie, I'm the real estate agent who sold the house to them. They bought the house from a police officer. He and his wife had one preschool son. Honey, that man was one of the worst fathers I've ever seen. The entire time we signed the closing papers he cursed and criticized that little fellow."

It appeared that the previous owners, when they didn't want to be bothered with him, had locked their little boy in his room. As author and speaker George Otis, Jr. often says, "In trauma the soul solicits many saviors." When that little boy was locked in the room, spirits of darkness befriended him. They can do that, you know. Demons will sometimes "minister" to you until you think you can count on them. Once they've sucked you in, they seek to destroy you (John 10:10).

The current owners reported that from that night forward their son slept soundly in that room.

The activities of the previous residents in your home could have lingering effects for you and your family. The real estate closing settles the issue of physical ownership. Spiritual ownership and authority, however, can be an entirely different matter.

One family discovered that from the moment they took ownership of their home, they were plagued with financial trouble. We asked, "Did you get the house at a good price?"

"Oh yes," the husband explained, "It was a foreclosure."

When they repented to God for the financial sins of the previous owners, breaking any curses on the property and consecrating it to the Lord, they experienced an immediate financial breakthrough.

The same is true of family abuse, violence, divorce and other relational sins committed by previous owners, which activate and release forces that defile the property. The forces can be expelled and their contracts with former owners annulled.

Houses, graveyards or "sacred groves" (places New Agers or witches deem to have special powers or which have been dedicated to demons) may at times require deliverance ministry, but need not be destroyed. What do you think? Could your home have similar problems?

Other Peoples' Property?

Suppose you have an unsaved roommate who has a collection of occult literature. Or perhaps you have an unsympathetic or lost family member who has possessions that dishonor God in the very house in which you live. What are you to do?

Clearly, you have no right to destroy or remove someone else's property. We suggest that you gather as many facts as possible beforehand and then appeal to them in love. Your presentation should be well thought-out and prepared. Don't base your request on superstition. We have too many superstitious Christians now. Base your request upon Scripture, your love for God, your respect for His presence and your desire to live under His protection and blessing. Pray and listen to God for His words of wisdom and direction before you attempt to make your case. Then do so with gentleness, love and respect.

Should that fail, then appeal to God. Ask the Lord to intervene on your behalf and also to provide protection for you. Remember that Moses was reared in Pharaoh's home and Joseph served in Potiphar's house in Egypt—both residences would have been filled with heathen worship artifacts. Yet both of these men were protected and mightily used of God!

When left with no alternatives, we can still live with God's blessing in any environment. We can purify our lives and possessions. We can purify our living spaces and announce to the enemy whose children we are and clearly delineate what does and what does not belong to us! In such cases, God counts us obedient (2 Cor. 8:12).

Parental Responsibilities

Parents, what about your children's possessions? When dealing with preschool children simply remove the offensive items. However, for older children it could provide an opportunity for you to explain the issues behind some of the toys, games and books that may be defiled. We parents should be sensitive and loving in any endeavor of this nature and not project mental images that provoke fear.

Of course, many children are sensitive to the Lord. They love God and want to please Him. Let's show them how to pray over their own possessions and decide what honors

Christ and what doesn't. Once they know the facts, many children take delight in ridding themselves of defilement.

As parents, each of us must decide how we will parent our children. We suggest that you first appeal to your children in love. Should that prove ineffective, then exercise your right as a parent and property owner. As property owners, we will simply not allow certain things to enter our homes. Please listen to God, then decide together what you will and will not allow. You will, as we have, draw a line somewhere. Will you allow just any type of music to be played in your home? Will you allow rock posters to be taped to your walls? Will you allow tobacco or illegal drug use in your home? Will you allow pornography? Are you going to permit premarital sex in your home? What about a satanic altar?

We have seen parents, at times, wrestle with each of these things in regard to their children. You too will draw a line somewhere! But remember, if you give the devil a toehold in your home, it will soon become a stronghold! Give the enemy an inch and he'll take a mile!

Effective Pollution Patrol

A father called us in a panic late one night. He said, "Eddie, I've just got to have your help. Our 17-year-old son is upstairs in his room right now. He's got heavy metal, acid rock music blaring, demonic rock-and-roll posters stapled to his walls, and he's up there right now smoking marijuana. What should I do?"

"Have you asked him to remove these things from his room?" I asked.

"Yes, but he won't do so," the father sheepishly replied.

"What he needs more than anything is a daddy," I said.

"I'm his daddy," he replied.

"No, sir, you're his father," I explained.

"A daddy establishes boundaries. Once your son violates the boundaries, go into the room, rip the posters off the wall, flush the marijuana down the toilet and remove the stereo! If that doesn't work, take his door off the hinges and store it in the garage. If he still doesn't get it, take his furniture out a piece at a time. When he's left with a blanket, a pillow and sleeps on the floor, he may get the point." A godly daddy will say, as Joshua did, "As for me and my house, we will serve the Lord" (Josh. 24:15).

Drastic tough love measures are rarely needed, thank God! But it may be helpful for your family to sit down together and decide what will be considered acceptable attitudes, behaviors and possessions in your home. You might even write a contract or covenant for both you and your children to sign. Do you agree with the plan of action we have presented? If not, how has God instructed you to handle this important issue?

Legalism and Superstition

If Satan can't convince us to keep things that defile our lives he will provoke us to legalism and superstition. In either case, he wins.

I (Alice) received a call from a woman who was obsessed with fear. I took a prayer team of ladies with me to visit in her home. We were absolutely shocked when we saw that she had pinned small prayer cloths to her curtains, her pictures, her bedspread, and even to her body!

"Where have you pinned prayer cloths to your body?" I asked. She raised her blouse; draped from her bra were several two-inch-square pieces of white cloth attached by safety pins.

"Is this all?" I quizzed her.

"No," she tentatively replied. She pulled her slacks halfway down to reveal a dozen or more cloths pinned around her panty line.

"Why are you doing this?" I asked.

"The television evangelist promised that they'd protect me from evil."

This lady had fallen to superstition. Our righteous living and the goodness of God is our protection—not a useless, worn-out piece of cloth.

Remember, we should be neither legalistic and judgmental nor fearful and superstitious. We should be discerning and, above all, seek God's will and direction in these matters. Don't rush to judgment!

Should we refuse to subscribe to the newspaper because it contains an astrological column or beer ad? Be sensible, be careful and, above all, be obedient. After all, "to obey is better than sacrifice" (1 Sam. 15:22). Pray and seek godly counsel if necessary. God tells us to "let the peace of God rule in your hearts" (Col. 3:15).

Prayer Assignment

Father God, I love You and would never want to dishonor You. I am excited about all You are teaching me right now. Your revelation is setting me free. Reveal to me any areas of my past that need repentance. (Wait for the Lord now.)

I am sorry for the wrong relationships I have entered into.
(Name each one.)

_____

_____

_____

_____

_____

_____

_____

Cleanse me now and set me free from any hold the enemy
has on me. Show me any object from a wrong relationship
that I need to discard, and I will do it. (Say aloud and with
your eyes open) Spirits of darkness, I break all unholy
soul ties between me and (make a list):

_____

_____

_____

_____

_____

_____

I cancel all sexual perversion through fornication, adultery,
pornography or mental lust in the name of Jesus. Heeding the
words of Matthew 3:10, I lay an ax to any unfruitful root of
darkness whether past or present. Thank You, Father, for
helping me. In Jesus' name I pray. Amen.

THE PURIFICATION PROCESS

In the Old Testament book of Leviticus, we read how the priests executed the rites of purification. Basically, they offered a sacrifice, anointed with oil, announced the cleansing and pronounced a blessing. Once purified, they were able to enter into God's will for them—to be sanctified.

> Sanctify yourselves therefore, and be ye holy: for I am the Lord your God. And ye shall keep my statutes, and do them: I am the Lord which sanctify you. And ye shall be holy unto me: for I the Lord am holy (Lev. 20:7-8, 26, *KJV*).

Reader, you are a priest and part of a kingdom of priests (Rev. 1:6)! Consecrate yourself to the Lord and heed His call to cleanse your life of defilement, as King Hezekiah did:

> "*Remove all defilement from the sanctuary.* Our fathers were unfaithful; they did evil in the eyes of the LORD. Therefore, the anger of the LORD has fallen on Judah and Jerusalem; he has made them an object of dread and

horror and scorn, as you can see with your own eyes. *This is why our fathers have fallen by the sword and why our sons and daughters and our wives are in captivity."* Then they went in to King Hezekiah and reported: "We have purified the entire temple of the LORD, the altar of burnt offering with all its utensils, and the table for setting out the consecrated bread, with all its articles. We have prepared and consecrated all the articles that King Ahaz removed in his unfaithfulness while he was king. They are now in front *of the LORD's altar"* (2 Chron. 29:5-6, 8-9,18-19, *NIV*, emphasis added).

An important key to our victory is for us to place our lives and our possessions "before the Lord's altar."

Put Away the Leaven!

Alice makes great homemade dinner rolls. My mouth waters when I think about them! To make her rolls rise and bake to their puffy perfection, she adds leaven (yeast). Leaven causes them to expand.

Sin is like leaven. It never remains the same; it always expands. Sin will take you further than you wanted to go, keep you longer than you intended to stay, and cost you more than you planned to pay. Sin is a God-given desire that is met in a God-forbidden way. It begins with a thought, develops into a feeling, and ultimately expresses itself in an action.

Leaven, in Scripture, represents sin, evil or false doctrine. For this reason the Lord called upon the Israelites to cleanse their homes of leaven, not just once but every year. Moses gave this instruction for the Israelites:

> And this day shall be unto you for a memorial; and ye shall keep it a feast to the LORD throughout your generations; ye shall keep it a feast by an ordinance for ever. Seven days shall ye eat unleavened bread; *even the first day ye shall put away leaven out of your houses:* for whosoever eateth leavened bread from the first day until the seventh day, that soul shall be cut off from Israel. And in the first day there shall be an holy convocation, and in the seventh day there shall be an holy convocation to you; no manner of work shall be done in them, save that which every man must eat, that only may be done of you. And ye shall observe the feast of unleavened bread; for in this selfsame day have I brought your armies out of the land of Egypt: therefore shall ye observe this day in your generations by an ordinance for ever. In the first month, on the fourteenth day of the month at even, ye shall eat unleavened bread, until the one and twentieth day of the month at even. *Seven days shall there be no leaven found in your houses:* for whosoever eateth that which is leavened, even that soul shall be cut off from the congregation of Israel, whether he be a stranger, or born in the land. Ye shall eat nothing leavened; in all your habitations shall ye eat unleavened bread (Exod. 12:14-20, *KJV*, emphasis added).

Each year in the Jewish home, the father would gather the family for this celebration. Before they began, he hid pieces of leavened bread in various places throughout the house to symbolize sin. Later during the celebration, the family members would search through the house for the hidden bits of leavened bread. The children especially enjoyed this traditional game.

As they found the bits of bread, the Jewish father would take a spoon, a dustpan and a feather and carefully sweep up each piece of leavened bread. After reading Scripture and praying together about hidden sin, the family would burn the leaven outside the house, symbolizing the removal of personal sin.

Remember, physical symbols often carry spiritual significance. For example, because Moses struck the rock twice, when God told him to strike it only once, he wasn't allowed to enter the Promised Land. Why? Well, it was more than simple disobedience; the rock represented Christ. Christ was stricken once for sin, not twice. So Moses had disrespected God's symbol!

Why Does the Church Lack Power?

When we fail to obey God, as Moses did, we too forfeit God's power in our lives. Our spiritual impotence should seriously concern us. Why do we lack power? Why is our authority over the enemy often compromised? Why does revival tarry?

Remember these lamentable words from Joshua 7:12-13 (emphasis added):

> Therefore *the children of Israel* could not stand before *their* enemies, but turned their backs before *their* enemies, because *they* have become doomed to destruction. Neither will I be with you anymore, unless you destroy the accursed from among you. Get up, sanctify the

people, and say, "Sanctify yourselves for tomorrow, because thus says the LORD God of Israel, '*There is an accursed thing in your midst, O Israel; you cannot stand before your enemies until you take away the accursed thing from among you.*' "

Israel's armies had defeated Jericho, but now their own security had been compromised. They were powerless and fearful. Verse 5 says, "The hearts of the people melted and became like water." Amazingly, that's the very same description of Israel's enemies just a few days earlier. The tables had been turned. Why were they fearful, intimidated and powerless against the enemies of God? Joshua wanted to know.

God gave him the answer: "Israel has sinned, and they have also transgressed My covenant which I commanded them. For they have even taken some of the accursed things . . . and they have also put it among their own stuff" (Josh. 7:11, emphasis added). Remember? One man—Achan—had taken prohibited items from Jericho and hidden them among his own possessions in his house. Because of this, the entire nation was crippled!

Just so, the Church today is crippled because Christ's people are overlooking a necessary key that unlocks the door to revival—to rid ourselves of corrupt things. Are there accursed things in your home? Deuteronomy 7:25-26 warns us that objects of idolatry, even silver or gold, could ensnare us:

You shall burn the carved images of their gods with fire; you shall not covet the silver or gold that is on them, nor take it for yourselves, lest you be snared by it; for it is an abomination to the Lord your God.

Nor shall you bring an abomination into your house, lest you be doomed to destruction like it. You shall utterly detest it and utterly abhor it, for it is an acursed thing.

The Seven Steps of Purification

Here are the steps God gave Joshua to take. Why don't you do them today?

1. Present Yourself to the Lord for His Inspection

Self-evaluation is insufficient. Why? Because "the heart is deceitful above all things, and desperately wicked; Who can know it?" (Jer. 17:9).

We must do as David did. We must present ourselves to God for His inspection. David prayed, "Search me, O God, and know my heart; try me, and know my anxieties; and see if there is any wicked way in me, and lead me in the way everlasting" (Ps. 139:23-24).

If we really are honest with this process, we can ask our Christian family and godly friends for their insight into our lives as well.

2. Sanctify Yourself

To sanctify ourselves is to set ourselves apart for God alone. The word "sanctify" is from the Hebrew word *qadash*, which means "to set apart from a profane to a sacred purpose."[1] We need to live sanctified lives before the Lord, put off the old and receive the new mandate to live in Christ.

As a deacon's wife divulged her daughter's involvement in Satanism, the Lord gave us what the Bible calls a word of knowledge, or spiritual impression (1 Cor. 12:8).

"Let's forget your daughter's Satanism for a moment," Alice said. "Tell us about your husband's pornography." Sure enough, her husband was deeply involved in pornography. He had opened the door to the demonic. Now demons were out to destroy his daughter's life!

In another situation, a deacon loaned his adult son one of his blank videocassettes to record a favorite television program. Several days later, as the son watched his taped show end, child pornography suddenly appeared on the screen. The revealing tape was one that his father wished later he had not grabbed in such haste. Numbers 32:23 says, "Be sure your sin will find you out."

In her book *The Voice of God*, author and teacher Cindy Jacobs writes:

What did Daniel do so God would release the people? He repented on their behalf, by admonishing, "We have sinned and committed iniquity" (v. 5). This kind of praying was also done by Ezra and Nehemiah and is called "identificational repentance."

Identificational repentance occurs when a person repents for the corporate sin of his or her nation. Does this mean that each person is not personally responsible before God for his or her own individual sins? Of course not. Each person must come to Christ for his or her own sins (John 3:16; Rev. 20:13).[2]

Sanctify yourself, your family and your possessions; and conduct necessary identificational repentance.

3. Locate the Offensive Items

Achan confessed that he had taken a beautiful Babylonian robe. Babylon, in Scripture, is said to be the seat of Satan or the center of evil in the earth. According to Ralph Woodrow, in his book *Babylon Mystery Religion*:

> Herodotus, the world traveler and historian of antiquity, witnessed the mystery religion and its rites in numerous countries and mentions how Babylon was the primeval source from which all systems of idolatry flowed. Bunsen says that the religious system of Egypt was derived from Asia and "the primitive empire in Babel."[3]

From the bounty of this pagan culture Achan had taken 200 shekels of silver and a wedge of gold weighing 50 shekels. "I coveted them," Achan said, "and took them" (Josh. 7:21). He loved those things more than he loved God. He desired their presence in his home more than he desired the Lord's presence. He admitted, "They are hidden in the ground inside my tent, with the silver underneath" (Josh. 7:21).

Are you willing to stand for holiness?

4. Rid Yourself of Those Things That Defile

Remove anything that relates to the occult, to heathen worship and to sin. The only solution is to remove them from the premises and destroy them completely, not give them away. These items attract demonic spirits and give them a right to inhabit your house. For you to fail to destroy these weapons of the enemy is to be an accomplice in his evil work (Jas. 4:17). That said, remember, we New Testament believers have neither the responsibility nor the right to destroy the property of others.

5. Be Serious About This

In the story of Joshua, once the Israelites obeyed the Lord and destroyed their spoils, His favor rested upon them again. Following their cleansing and repentance, Israel utterly destroyed the city of Ai along with its king! No enemy could stand before them!

You may think, *This is the Old Testament. What does it have to do with me, today?* Paul explained, "Now *all these things happened unto them for examples:* and *they are written for our admonition*, upon whom the ends of the world are come. Wherefore let him that thinketh he standeth take heed lest he fall" (1 Cor. 10:11-12, *KJV*, emphasis added). If the demands of holiness were that great under the law, how much greater they must be under grace.

6. Renounce the Enemy and Your Association with Him

Break any contracts and unholy ties you have made with darkness, whether you made them knowingly or unknowingly. Speak aloud: "I break any and all unholy soul ties that I made while in my ungodly relationship with _____ (name the person or sin). I sever these ties now in the name of Jesus, and take back any ground I gave the enemy in committing that sin." Repeat this process for each item or, in some cases, each person.

7. Consecrate Your Life and Property to the Glory of the Lord

Some Christians choose to anoint their houses with oil, which is symbolic of the Holy Spirit. We call that a "prophetic act."

Prophetic acts are recorded in Josh. 5:2-3, 8-9; 6:1-17; Jer. 13:1-11; 19:1-15; Ezek. 3:1-7; 4:1-8. We can't say whether or not a prophetic act is necessary. The important thing is to follow the leadership of the Holy Spirit. Each of us should seek God's guidance in each situation.

Jesus created stories (called parables) to communicate His teaching points. Learn from this parable we've created for you.

The Parable of Bill and Mary

Bill and Mary had been married for many years. Their kids were grown and no longer lived at home. Mary was a committed Christian, but Bill lived without Christ. His whole life revolved around his business.

One week, Mary's church was having an evangelistic crusade. She convinced Bill to attend the Sunday evening service with her. To make him more comfortable, they sat near the back of the auditorium. As the evangelist completed his message, he invited the audience to receive Christ. Bill suddenly experienced something unfamiliar, as if God's finger had touched his heart. He felt exposed, unnerved, vulnerable—even lost. He listened to the story of Christ's death on Calvary and was overwhelmed by his own wickedness. He stumbled to the front of the auditorium and tearfully confessed his sin. He repented and invited Jesus Christ into his life and was wonderfully saved. Bill was a brand-new man! Mary and her friends were ecstatic! They had prayed for Bill's salvation for years.

That night Mary and Bill were almost asleep when Bill's heart was abruptly gripped by guilt. He tried to escape it, but he couldn't. He turned over and tearfully said, "Mary, I have something I need to confess to you."

"Are you referring to Janet?" Mary asked.

"Yes," Bill confirmed, "but how do you know about Janet and me?"

"Bill, I've known about your affair for two years," she replied.

Bill was amazed. "Honey, I've sinned against both you and God. Can you ever find it in your heart to forgive me?"

Mary smiled, gently caressed his chin and said, "Sweetheart, tonight God forgave you of all your sins. I love you, and of course I forgive you." Bill fell fast asleep with a peace he had never known.

The next day Bill left for work. He was born again! It really was like the birth of a new life. He stopped on the way home from work to pick up flowers to take to Mary. He couldn't believe the warmth of their new Christ-centered relationship. *Why had he waited so long?* He wondered.

Tuesday morning he called home and invited Mary to meet him for lunch. The newness Christ had brought to their marriage was wonderful! Bill and Mary were experiencing genuine spiritual unity; and after all these years they were on the same page. Why, he felt newly wed!

Wednesday morning Bill was interrupted by his secretary's voice over the intercom. "Bill," she announced, "Janet is here to see you." It was as if Bill's blood had turned to iced water. *Oh, no! It's Janet!* he thought. Then it dawned on him that he had made everything right with God and with Mary, but he had forgotten to break his sinful relationship with Janet.

Do you get the point? It's important that we break off our former relationships with the enemy. He's lawless, rebellious and relentless. He'll do anything he can to ruin our Kingdom effectiveness. Until Bill faced Janet and announced it was over between them, Janet would continue to pursue Him. It's time for us to say to the enemy, "Enough is enough. It's over!" The devil knows that the best way to hinder our effectiveness is to work against our new relationship with Christ. Deal ruthlessly with Satan! Renounce his work. Remove his opportunities to hurt you, and start anew! Jesus said, "The kingdom of heaven has been forcefully advancing, and forceful men lay hold of it" (Matt. 11:12, *NIV*).

If you will put these principles into practice, we are "confident of this very thing, that He who has begun a good work in you will complete it until the day of Jesus Christ" (Phil. 1:6).

Prayer Assignment

Lord, thank You that what You have begun in me You will complete. I receive Your freedom and I will walk in the victory You've given to me in obedience to You.
I love You, Jesus. Amen!

Notes

1. Finis Jennings Dake, *Dake's Annotated Reference Bible*, as referenced from Exodus 13:2 (Lawrenceville, GA: Dake Bible Sales, 1963), p. 77.
2. Cindy Jacobs, *The Voice of God* (Ventura, CA: Regal Books, 1995), p. 241.
3. Ralph Woodrow, *Babylon Mystery Religion* (Riverside, CA: Ralph Woodrow Evangelistic Association, Inc., 1966), p. 10.

PART TWO

❖

STORIES AND
APPLICATIONS

HOME-FRONT STORIES OF SPIRITUAL HOUSECLEANING

In America today, TV shows on home improvement reveal how consumers collectively spend millions each year on everything from bathrooms to blinds, landscaping to light fixtures, all in attempts to create the perfect look and atmosphere for their homes. Sadly, much of the interior décor Christians buy to create this "perfect look" in their homes includes crystal pyramids, Buddhist picture plaques, gold-leaf dragon coffee tables, sphinx heads and religious icons from around the world.

But a new coat of paint for your home has far less to do with a home's true environment than do the elements inside and out. How is the spiritual environment inside your home? Is your home illuminated by the light of Christ or dimmed by spiritual darkness? Is it a place of peace or panic? Do you run to your home as a refuge or run from your home because of the inexplicable oppression you feel within it?

In this chapter, we share the stories of those who cleaned house on a deeply spiritual (and profoundly practical) level. We look at why different residents experienced nightmares and insomnia, unemployment and illness, ghostly appearances and bizarre manifestations that provoked fear and frustration in their lives. We reveal how various objects and activities opened the door to the demonic forces behind those things. These stories examine what lie at the root of each experience and expose the enemy's tactics for staking a squatter's claim in a home. We also give you biblical tools with which you can evict these unseen tenants from your home.

Sensations, Smells and Sleepless Nights

Spiritual housecleaning can change a home's physical environment. Sue White tells the following story about how this affected her home:

> This story takes place back in the early '90s when writing books was just a glint in Eddie's and Alice's eyes. Alice had helped us find a foreclosed home in Houston, Texas, in a nice neighborhood across the road from our children's school and a short drive from our church.
>
> Things couldn't have been better until we noticed some strange happenings in our home. An odd odor would drift out of the air conditioning vent in our master bedroom, and the temperature in Robin, our oldest daughter's bedroom was considerably colder than the other rooms in the house. We tried to dismiss these issues as "normal"—perhaps a mouse or bird had died in

our attic, releasing the putrid odor—but on a regular basis? Aren't there always rooms in a house that have uneven airflow, creating cold spots? Our thought was to close the air vent a bit and warm the room a few degrees—right? Well, not so in this case.

Eddie was the associate pastor at our church; Alice was an awesome Bible teacher and intercessor. We learned about deliverance, spiritual mapping and spiritual housecleaning from their teachings. It amazed us to learn that spiritual entities could take residence in people, inanimate objects and buildings. By now, our teenage daughter also had difficulty sleeping and would awake with nightmares. We felt it was worth checking the possibility that our house had some unwanted "guests" in residence, so I called Eddie to discuss my suspicions and scheduled him to come pray through our home.

Eddie arrived on schedule and walked through our home. He didn't immediately indicate his feelings, but patiently listened as I explained the unusual things we'd experienced. Then he carefully explained the process. We would pray through each room, trusting the Lord to point out anything that displeased Him. We'd remove whatever He revealed. Then Eddie would pray a blessing over our home and family. What unfolded next was amazing!

In the dining room near the front entrance, Eddie received a revelation that there was something "dark" in there. He told us that he never "saw" demons, though he sometimes sensed or felt their presence. God gave him a word of knowledge that the previous owner's son had played the occult game *Dungeons and Dragons* in the dining room with his friends, and that several spirits had been given "legal right" to lurk there. Eddie rebuked the evil spirits and sent them packing! As a follow-up to Eddie's visit I interviewed some of my neighbors who knew the previous owners of our home, and they confirmed that the teenage son played *D&D* in that room during most of his waking hours!

We progressed to the master bedroom where the putrid odor—the smell of something dead—would appear. Strangely, we didn't smell anything unpleasant outside that room. Eddie rebuked whatever was causing the odor and announced that they no longer had permission to invade our home. From that moment, the awful odor never returned.

Lastly, we arrived at our daughter's bedroom. Did I mention that my husband was an air-conditioning technician and had done all of the normal tricks to the thermostat, air vents and air conditioning unit in an attempt to balance the temperature in her room? For some unknown reason, Eddie focused on the closed clothes closet. He said, "Sue, there's something right here that seems to be causing the problem."

He couldn't see any of its contents until we opened the door and looked through the items near the area he'd identified. A jewelry box sat on a shelf at that spot. We opened the box and sorted through its contents.

There were a number of pieces of costume jewelry and trinkets that Robin had collected. One necklace seemed to draw Eddie's attention. It had a crystal-looking pendant with the image of a Chinese pagoda etched into it.[1] It had sentimental value. My father had bought it for my mother years before during a visit to San Francisco. My mother thought it would be nice for Robin to have a remembrance of her grandfather. Eddie felt strongly that this item had caused the disturbance. He suggested that since it had sentimental value we first try moving the necklace out to the garage to see if anything changed in the bedroom. If things improved, then a decision would have to be made as to what to do about it.

Within hours the temperature changed in that room, and in the nights that followed, our daughter's sleep was not interrupted again by nightmares. We prayed about it as a family and decided to throw the necklace in the trash rather than give it back to my mother. It made no sense to shift our problem to another location and allow the demonic spirits an opportunity to bother someone else.

At last we were rid of the foul spirits that had troubled our home. Eddie's prayer of blessing was wonderful, and our subsequent visitors would often remark about how restful our home was. Our eyes were opened to the power of prayer and the need for spiritual housecleaning.

Prayer Prevails Over a "Haunted House"

Connie Jost from Texas shares this story about a house that she and her family lived in when she was a child:

When I was eight years old (children are the enemy's easiest target), our family of seven lived in a very small, cramped house. My mother began to pray earnestly for a larger house. Looking through the ads in our local paper, she noticed an offer from another family to trade a large, old house for a smaller house. She fell in love with this house, built in 1910, a large two-story house in a quaint neighborhood. Amazingly, they traded houses with us for a small difference in price.

Ours was a conservative Christian Mennonite family. My parents were moral and intelligent—nothing strange about us. So when we began to notice strange things and tell our friends, they didn't doubt our veracity but really didn't believe what we observed.

As children we loved this house—with both a front and back set of stairs—in which we could play the game "Hide and Seek." One night when my sister and I were left alone, we heard a loud crash overhead and what sounded like a strong wind blowing through the house. We ran upstairs to check, but all the windows were closed and nothing appeared amiss. This happened three times before we ran to the neighbor's house and he returned to the house with us. When my parents came home, the neighbor gave them a look and a wink and said, "They heard something."

I was terrified of the dark and began to experience terrible nightmares every night, which I accepted as normal. There was a dark presence in the house that I could feel. This presence began to manifest itself to various members of our family, usually with the sound of heavy footsteps across the hall upstairs and then descending the back stairs. We heard doors slam and water running, and when we looked, the door was locked and no water was evident.

One time when our family went on vacation, two male friends house sat: One was an ex-motorcycle gang member and one was an ex-Marine who had served in Vietnam. When we arrived home from our vacation, they said they wouldn't spend another night at our house again! They reported that in the middle of the night they heard footsteps cross the hall, slowly descend the back stairs and come up to the door of the family room. The steps then turned and went back up.

My father, an engineer, was entirely skeptical of the rest of us. One Sunday morning he had a bad migraine headache and stayed at home in bed while the rest of us went to church. About noon, he heard the side door slam and heard our voices and the sound of chairs sliding up to the dining room table. When he went down to say "Hi," he found the doors locked and the house empty. We walked in a moment later and he was white as a sheet.

A humorous thing happened one night as my mother waited for my teenage brother to come home. As midnight approached, she heard the back door open and close and then the bathroom door close loudly. She walked over, and sure enough the door was locked and she pulled it with some force. Keeping an eye on the door, she walked back to the living room and whispered loudly, "Wally! Wally! There's an intruder." My father came down with his rifle, walked to the bathroom door and flung it open. No one was there. My father was holding my crying mother with the rifle in his hand when my brother walked in and said, "I promise I'll never come home late again!"

My worst experience was when I was a freshman in college. I came home one night to find the house dark. My own dog barked and snarled at me and bared his teeth. I made it past him and felt the usual fear descend on me as I busied myself and washed my hair in the kitchen sink. I heard a loud click, and I looked up to see the light cord swinging rapidly back and forth, as if someone had thrown it. Terrified, I went back upstairs to my bedroom and switched on the radio loudly to drown out any sounds. When I heard my mother call my name, I switched off the radio, ran to the top of the stairs and yelled, "What?" relieved that someone was home, but I was met with silence. This happened three times. In desperation I called my girlfriend. The static on the line was so loud I had to yell. "What did you say? I can't hear you!" she yelled back. I hung up. Fortunately, my parents came home shortly after.

We'd lived with these frightening experiences for nine years when we visited a family friend's church. He was their pastor. He said he didn't know why, but he felt impressed to preach from a passage in the Old Testament about having nothing to do with mediums, sorcerers, astrologers or witchcraft. Feeling certain that these noises we heard were demonic, we searched out a missionary from Brazil who told us to renounce it (aloud), and cleanse our house in Jesus' name.

My father prayed throughout the house in Jesus' name, commanding the spirits of darkness to leave, and we noticed a very definite change. The house became silent, and that sense of fear lifted. Since that day, my dreams have been pleasant.

The previous owners of the house had a son who became a friend of my brother's. He later admitted, "We heard strange things all the time in that house." (That's why it was such a great bargain!) Yet those experiences taught me to identify the presence of evil and how to stand against it and prevail in prayer.

Cleansing a House of Witchcraft

April, a friend from Ohio, shares a similar story about how she prayed over her house and asked God to cleanse it from the witchcraft that had been performed there:

We were so excited when we started looking at houses to buy, as our home is ministry headquarters. (No wonder the enemy attacks it and seeks to infiltrate it!) We had been asking the Lord for the right timing and to find us a house where He wanted us to minister.

When we found the house, I was somewhat apprehensive. It might have had something to do with a dream I had about the house. After visiting this house, I dreamed of a snake on one of the cabinets in the kitchen. I wasn't afraid, just upset, and in the dream I asked the Lord what it meant. Then I saw a rainbow cover the back of the snake and I heard the Lord say, "I am giving you this house, but you will have to fight for it (not unlike the Promised Land)." So we went forward and the Lord opened one door after another.

Soon after we moved in, we had our pastor and his wife over. Together we prayed and dedicated our home to the Lord for His service. As we prayed, I sensed something was spiritually wrong in the house. Instead of disrupting our gathering, I felt like the Lord said to be patient, that He would uncover things in His timing. So we dedicated the home and ourselves to Him for all He desired. (Note: Some feel that when they rent or purchase a property and later discover it's defiled, that they've somehow missed God and made a mistake. They haven't learned that God, who is reconciling all things to Himself, often moves us onto land and into property to bring it back under His Lordship!)

We'd been taught spiritual housecleaning early in our Christian lives, and had learned to discern the atmosphere in our home, but this was another level for us. The Lord revealed that high-level witchcraft had been practiced in our home. Three different neighbors confirmed it. This was significant, because Scripture teaches that things are to be established by two or three witnesses (Matt. 18:16).

Our two closest neighbors told us that the previous residents, professed witches, offered sacrifices in the backyard. The neighbors who live behind us explained that a witch coven met between our house and theirs. Their landlord was planning to tear down their house because the decaying animal bones attracted termites. This explained why our dog was continually finding bones in the yard.

We attended a deliverance conference where we learned that we were now clean in Christ and should, for that reason, keep our house clean. We gathered the family (spiritual housecleaning is a family affair), put on praise music and our three daughters read the Word and worshipped while we went from room to room, asking the Lord to bring revelation of anything unpleasing that we—and the previous owners—had brought into the house.

We went through the house, top to bottom. We repented on behalf of the previous owners (identificational repentance) and took authority in Jesus' name. We asked the Lord to remove every defiled thing and to apply the precious blood of Jesus in its place (Neh. 1:4-7; Ps. 106:4-8).

Since then, we've become even more sensitive to the spiritual atmosphere in our house. When we share our testimony of victory, people often ask us to come help clean their homes. If the Lord allows us to go, we use it as a tool to teach them what God taught us about how to maintain the spiritual atmosphere in our home.

Ungodly Clutter

In the following story, I (Alice) explain how one couple made a clean sweep of religious icons and idols inside their home. After we identified the problems and gave the couple instructions on what to do, within weeks, their health, finances and circumstances completely changed.

I was in our office when a call came in from a woman who lives in our city. She and her husband had read *Spiritual Housecleaning* and felt they needed help.

She said, "My husband, Calvin, and I are both sick. We are one week away from our house going into foreclosure, and we have a completely renovated townhouse that we've not been able to rent for three years. We are dealing with two unjust lawsuits, no work is coming in, and we are $50,000 behind in taxes. We read your book, but there are so many things wrong with our home, we don't know what to do. Can you help us?"

"Where do you live?" I asked.

"Just off the freeway," was her reply.

I sensed the Lord say that I was to take a team of women to their house and pray, so we set the appointment. I called my weekly prayer team and they agreed to join me at Calvin and Sandi's house for our regular Wednesday morning prayer time.

The house was a typical Houston home with a large yard filled with many old oak trees beautifully draped in Spanish moss. The yards in the neighborhood were nicely manicured for older homes, but our new friends' home was a different story. They too would have admitted that the front yard and driveway looked as if a perpetual garage sale had been going on. There were flatbed trailers filled with street lamps, barbecue equipment and other miscellaneous things. But the front of their house was only a preview of what was inside.

When we entered their house, Calvin and Sandi graciously introduced themselves to each of us, and we visited for a few minutes. It wasn't hard to see why they were so overwhelmed. There was clutter and chaos from corner to corner.

Calvin and Sandi told us that the Worshipful Master of the Masonic Lodge (located two blocks away) had built the home more than three decades before. Many Masonic meetings had been conducted in their home while waiting for the lodge to be built. The wife had named the middle room "the devil's den" because that's where she smoked her cigarettes and drank her wine. All the neighbors knew about her room. But the disturbing part is that when the home was sold to the second family, the teenage son's room was the middle bedroom. He was a very troubled teen whom friends said "dedicated the house to the devil," and he was obsessed with Marilyn Manson's music. Calvin and Sandi were the third owners but they hadn't heard of spiritual housecleaning before reading our book. Yet they knew something was very wrong with their home.

After a time of prayer, our intercessory prayer team moved from room to room to see what the Lord might say. Every room had crucifixes (representations of Jesus hanging dead on the cross). Some were in drawers, some were visible and some were in jewelry boxes. I asked

Sandi about this, and she told me that her background was Catholic, even though she was now born again and a faithful member of a wonderful non-denominational church. Her mother, a strict adherent of praying to Mary, had continued to give her pictures of Mary and crucifixes all different one from the other. Out of respect, she had kept them all. (See information about Catholic icons in chapter three, "What Constitutes Defilement.")

We found Masonic emblems, scores of crucifixes, coffee cups with zodiac symbols on them and questionable movies and pictures. Just walking through the cluttered house was a challenge for my team; but as we prayed and broke contracts along the way, especially in the second bedroom, the Spirit of God was more and more obviously present with us.

One of our prayer-team felt led to pray for Calvin and Sandi's physical healing. God showed up in a powerful way. Standing in the kitchen, both Calvin and Sandi almost collapsed into our arms! I instructed them to clean their home one room at a time and to pray over each room, dedicating it to the Lord and His glory. I reminded them of the steps outlined in our book. Calvin and Sandi appeared excited and motivated.

Two weeks later I called Sandi. "How's it going?" I asked, praying that she had taken my advice.

"Oh, my goodness, you won't believe it, Alice! We've thrown away so much stuff that our neighbors continue to come to the door and ask if we are moving. Both of the lawsuits that were against us have been supernaturally dismissed and one of our clients has paid his bill of over $1,000. Our house won't go into foreclosure because God has provided the three months of back payments that were due. And yesterday morning three people called to ask if they could rent our townhouse. The biggest shock was that two of the potential renters literally raced to our door to get the contract first. Our teenage daughter is so excited about our spiritual housecleaning that instead of visiting with her friends, she decided to stay home just to help us. We feel lighter with every bag full of trash and all the dishonorable things we've thrown out. We still have a lot to do, but after the first day of cleaning, my business phone finally rang again. And Calvin's knee is so much better. Call me back in a couple more weeks, once we're finished."

A week later, I got a surprise call from Sandi. "You know our back taxes? Well, I called the IRS and they have agreed to work out a payment plan that we can handle. Before now they were rude and unreasonable, all I could do was cry in discouragement."

One month later I called Sandi. With incredible excitement Sandi said, "Our house is so clean. I found dozens of crucifixes and unbelievable junk that we didn't even realize we had kept from our 'ungodly days.' We're sleeping soundly now and our aches and pains are very few. It's remarkable the miracles we have experienced."

"But I must tell you about the final night," Sandi continued. "I was about to fall asleep, when I heard the

Holy Spirit say to me, 'Sandi, you missed a crucifix. It's caught in the back of your jewelry box.' I sat up in the bed, amazed. I realized that it had been years since I had heard the voice of the Holy Spirit so clearly. I got up and walked over to my standing jewelry case. Bending over, I pulled each drawer out to peer into the back where the crucifix might have been caught. To my surprise, there it was, just as the Lord had said. I reached in and pulled out a crucifix necklace that had been snagged on the felt-lined back wall of the case. This crucifix, a European version, was particularly gory, as Jesus looked so gaunt and defeated. I repented to the Lord, threw it away and broke all contracts with death that had for so long filled our home. I slept like a baby that night. *We are free, free, free!*"

Six years after this happened I called Calvin to ask him to do some carpentry work for us. I asked, "How are you guys doing?"

Calvin answered, "We're absolutely great! I can't stay on top of all the business that is coming in, and in fact I can't get to the work you want done for another two weeks. And the same is true for Sandi. We are almost completely debt-free, except for the taxes, but that is coming along well, too. We are healthy, our home is clean, and we are truly grateful for *Spiritual Housecleaning*. It saved our lives."

Whew! What a huge weight was lifted from Sandi's and Calvin's shoulders! It must have been like being born again, again!

Humility is vital if we are to receive help from the Holy Spirit and others. Perhaps you've cried out to God for help before but have been reluctant to let go of your possessions and your pride as well. If so, and if you're now willing to change, take a moment and humble yourself before God and repent for your stubbornness. As we humbly submit to God, we'll receive the help we need to be free from spiritual bondage. Perhaps your house is not as bad as Calvin and Sandi's, but even the tidiest home can collect spiritual clutter. Something as simple as a teacup, a toy, a piece of jewelry or a DVD can have significant impact on an otherwise spiritually clean home.

Don't hesitate! Like Calvin and Sandi, choose humility and take action to get free now!

Possessed Painting

Sometimes, the gifts that people give us can invite a demonic presence into our homes. Mary Martinez from Texas shares the following story of how a painting she was given created havoc in her home:

Several years ago, a friend gave me a painting as a going-away gift. My friend's husband had painted the picture, so it was very special. This young man loved to read and study the history of Native American spirituality. He had large collections of books and artifacts. Of course I took the painting. I had no idea it could potentially open a door for demonic activity in my home.

Our son liked Native American things, so when we moved into our new home, I hung it in his room. About two months later, my son started talking in his sleep very loudly—something he hadn't done before. So my husband and I decided to pray over our home. For a while the sleep talking stopped, but it wasn't very long afterward that not only was he talking but he also started sleepwalking. He gave us quite a scare one night when he unlocked his bedroom door that faced the backyard and ran around the outside of the house screaming. He ran to the front of the house and banged on the front door, not knowing where he was. When my husband and I woke up, opened the front door and asked him how he got there, he said, "I don't know."

The following day, I went to his room to pray. I asked the Lord what in his room was causing all these things to happen. I prayed again and heard God softly say that I was to study the Indian painting. This picture was of a warrior Indian on a horse. At the base, where the hoofs of the horse were, was a dead carcass of a buffalo and on the left thigh of the horse was a red handprint.

When I looked at the painting, in the holes where the eyes of the dead carcass used to be, I saw two demonic, peering eyes, red as the color of blood. An ugly, cold chill ran all over my body. I knew that I had to get rid of the painting. I asked the Lord what that was and He told me that demons can possess anything and hide anywhere and go unnoticed for a long time. So I removed the painting from the wall and trashed it. I prayed and anointed our home. Our son had peace in his room, and all demonic activity ceased.

This is not to suggest that Indians are demonic or that all the things they make are evil. I own some beautiful Native American paintings and love them and their culture. I understand now that it was a spirit behind that painting that empowered it and created fear. It's what we believe in. The young man who painted the picture, like us, didn't understand spiritual contracts with darkness, or that he had an open door in his life that activated the demonic realm through his art. *Praise God we are free.*

Evil Slips in Through the Pages of a Magazine

In this brief testimony, Sheri from Houston shares how spiritual housecleaning freed her from freakish dreams and restless nights:

For years demonic dreams tormented me. In these dreams I battled with demons and would awake hoarse from screaming, "In Jesus' name, you must go!" This was ongoing almost nightly.

As I began spiritual housecleaning, the Lord brought me to a magazine advertisement that I had cut out years earlier and had hanging on my desk cabinet at the foot of my bed. It contained an inspirational photo of an amputee running with one leg and a prosthesis—with a tennis shoe attached to it. It said, "Run your race and do not quit," and something about the heart of a champion. It certainly inspired me!

I tried to be sensitive to the voice of the Holy Spirit, and as I picked up the picture and turned it over, the hair on my arms stood straight up! I immediately felt sick to my stomach. To my surprise there was a picture of a demon used to advertise the release of the movie *Spawn of Satan*. Needless to say, I prayed as I tore it in pieces. To this day I'm no longer tormented in my dreams! *Hallelujah!*

Only as we seek discernment and wisdom from the Lord will we be able to effectively clean house. To do anything less is to operate out of the flesh (our lower Adamic nature) in a spirit of suspicion, superstition and paranoia—and that's not what God wants. He came to give us abundant Christian life (John 10:10)!

If you're troubled by nightmares, experience demonic attacks or feel something oppressive in your home, ask the Lord to reveal to you the root of the oppression. He is faithful. He has the answers you need to free you from fear and oppression.

In the Least Likely Places

Rose asked the Lord to reveal the root of the oppression that lingered in her home. She had cleaned house but still found it hard to pray, so she asked the Lord to uncover any spiritually dark and offensive things still hidden in her home. She wrote to us and described her experience:

> I read your book *Spiritual Housecleaning* because I found it very difficult to pray in my newly purchased town-home. Previously I had several friends pray through my house and conduct spiritual housecleaning but there was still a hindrance.
>
> After reading your book, I asked the Holy Spirit to uncover any ungodly thing we missed. A few days later,

I asked some workers who were in my attic to tell me if any boxes or items were in the attic that weren't part of my small cluster of stored boxes. The workmen found a box that they brought down to me. Inside the unfamiliar box was an Aztec god chess set and books on the paranormal. I was shocked! They must have been left by the previous owners.

To find that junk was an answer to my prayers. I broke all contracts with these items and my home, and asked the Lord's blessing.

Does this mean that we're to turn our houses upside down in search of potentially dangerous hidden objects? Are we bound to suffer needlessly because of devilish trinkets that other people left behind? Obviously, the answer is no. Isaiah 54:17 says, "No weapon forged against you will prevail" (*NIV*). As believers, we have the power to discern and overcome the plots and schemes of the evil one. But we should ask the Lord to reveal them to us. When we don't ask, we don't receive. And there are times the devil will take advantage of our ignorance if we're not observant (2 Cor. 2:11).

But my things are innocent, you might think. *Why would God want me to get rid of things that make me happy or that have sentimental value?* But seemingly innocent, "fun" interests, activities and objects, as we'll see in the next testimony, can sometimes lead us into temptation and torment.

What Are You Watching?

In the following story, a man named Chuck told us how he was able to trace his angry attitude back to violent movies:

I remember when your book came out. I had received my copy but had not read it. After all, I didn't have anything in my house or life that needed cleaning up—or so I thought. My Lord had already begun a wonderful work in my life and had brought me a long way from where I had been. But I thought, *Could there be anything else that needed attention?*

It was fall of 2003. My wife had gone to see her mother and I had the weekend alone. The Lord had dealt with me about total commitment, so it was good to be alone, pray and seek His will in my life.

Friday evening as I prayed, I had a strong impression to read *Spiritual Housecleaning.* I said, "Well, all right, Lord, if that's what You want." As I read, I learned many things I hadn't known, things that have helped me understand circumstances that come to me as prayer assignments. But that wasn't the reason I was supposed to read this book. The Lord had something very special for me that evening. One simple phrase changed my life for eternity.

Eddie and Alice listed "sources of defilement." As I read the list, I felt a bit smug and self-righteous. None of those things were in my life. I turned the page and casually read each line almost saying out loud, "That's not me."

Until I read the line "movies with occult messages, extreme violence." I think my heart skipped a beat and I read it again—"extreme violence." I said, "But I love violent movies, the more violent the better."

That's when God began speaking to me. "Do you love these things more than Me?"

"No! You know that I love You more than any movie, Lord."

That evening I told God that He is first in my life and if violent movies displeased Him, I would not watch them. But wouldn't you know it; the enemy saw this as an opportunity to tempt me. I didn't know there were so many violent movies. It seemed like a new one was released every time I turned on the TV.

Why wouldn't Jesus allow me to watch those kinds of movies? At first I didn't understand. But I learned long ago that the Lord has a purpose for my life, and when I don't understand, I'm simply to trust Him.

My Lord has made me a tenderhearted and compassionate man, with mercy as one of my spiritual gifts. I now understand that those violent movies were destroying what God wanted to do in me. There was a time when I had the emotions of a stone and the compassion of a wild hog. Now God has changed all that, and He's given me a tender heart. I can now cry for the lost and dying world. My life now is better because of what Jesus has done. Thank You, Lord!

Again, this is not about superstition, paranoia or legalism. This is about obedience and honoring God with all of our heart, soul, mind and strength (Deut. 6:5; Mark 12:30)—and our possessions. It's about having lives and homes that leave no room for the devil to get a foothold. God wants to establish environments of light, peace and joy in our areas of influence.

Burning Bridges from the Devil

A modern-day example of what happened in the City of Ephesus, in Acts 19:17-20, took place in a rural part of Illinois when a former Wicca high priestess stumbled on our book *Spiritual Housecleaning*. She tells the following story:

I was walking around the Christian bookstore praying earnestly for the Holy Spirit to lead me to a book that would help and encourage me. What an answer to prayer when I spotted a thin blue book entitled *Spiritual Housecleaning*. This powerful little book confirmed what the Holy Spirit had done in my life over the previous year.

Fourteen years ago, I became a rebellious pastor's daughter and turned my back on God for 10 long years. One day I discovered the New Age section in a bookstore. I picked up a book on magic just for fun and followed the author's directions. To my amazement, it worked! I tried another spell, then another and soon I was hooked!

Soon after, I bought my first set of Tarot Cards and read fortunes for many people. I hungered more and more for the supernatural. I searched the Internet and found a group of Wiccans (witches) who were 30 miles away and had a wonderful metaphysical store where I could purchase all of my magical supplies.

I joined them and quickly earned the title of High Priestess. But something was missing. I remember sitting outside one day, saying to myself, *Is this it? Is this all there is to Wicca? Where are the so-called ancient mysteries?* All I'd been taught was garbage. Good old Satan, the master deceiver, had stolen 10 years of my life and filled me with empty, false religion, but I kept plugging away, hoping it would get better. Instead I only became emptier and angrier.

One January, as I flipped through the television channels I stopped on a Christian broadcast. I can't tell you who the preacher was or what the message was—I just realized how much I needed Jesus! I turned off the TV, knelt beside my couch and cried out to God. He forgave me and freed me from the occult!

I knew that I needed to get rid of all of my occult things. A few days later, I went to the burn barrel on our farm and burned books, wands, staffs, robes, herbs and other paraphernalia.

Wow! I don't know the value of the items I burned that day; it was more than I care to recall.

I held on to a few things that I wasn't quite willing to part with, namely my Tarot Cards. How I loved and depended on them for all my answers! God dealt with me on this matter. I told Him, "Lord, I love You and thank You for setting me free, but I love my cards, I need them. I've read the Bible all the way through many times, Lord, but it didn't do much for me. So, Lord, until You make the Bible come alive to me like these cards, I cannot part with them."

The God of the universe loved me so much that He actually heard and answered my ignorant prayer. I began to read my Bible regularly, and to my surprise the Word of God came alive to me! He gave me detailed answers unlike anything the cards had ever given me. About a month later I said, "Lord! Do You realize that I haven't picked up my cards in about a month? I've only trusted Your Word!" And the Lord said, "Yes, now burn them."

I obediently bundled up and headed out on that blizzard morning to my burn barrel. The cards took a long time to burn. I believe God made the winds flip each card one at a time and hit the side of the barrel and then slowly melt. The meaning of each card went through my mind as I watched them melt and the grotesque yellowy-black smoke rise into the sky. I shivered as I waited for the last card to melt and disappear. Then I walked away.

When I reached the other side of my farmhouse, I noticed that the snow had stopped falling and the sun was out. The beautiful field of freshly fallen snow sparkled like a million small diamonds and my Savior whispered, "Michelle, this is your heart now. I have washed it as white as this snow. You are free!"

I speak from experience when I say, "Spiritual housecleaning is the key to true freedom!"

Breaking Ungodly Covenants

In 2 Samuel 21:1-14, David—and the entire nation of Israel—had a serious problem. Having suffered through three years of famine, the king was desperate for the reason why. When he cried out to God for the answer, the Lord revealed the reason His people were in such a dire situation: Sins of the past—sins that David and the current generation were likely unaware of—

had defiled and brought the wrath of God upon the land. Although it may seem strange to us, when David learned this, he took immediate action to rectify the wrongs Israel had committed and to make right a broken promise.

These kinds of accounts aren't limited to what we read in Scripture. Current, real-life examples of those who've cleaned house God's way come to us all the time. Here, a young man writes to tell us how he used the principles he learned from *Spiritual Housecleaning* to break free from an ungodly covenant and from the chains of Satanism and suicide:

I first heard about spiritual housecleaning in May 2005 and I knew that I needed to do it. As I prayed, the Lord showed me things. At this time I was very bound by Satan, having been a Satanist for many years. I was on 16 different psychiatric meds at the time and constantly wanted to kill myself. I felt that there was no hope and that no one wanted me. The Lord showed me that cleaning house was the next step in my freedom.

As I did spiritual housecleaning, the first thing I came across was blood from a blood covenant that I had made with my brother before he died. I could not let go of him. After I destroyed the vial of blood, I was no longer plagued with evil thoughts of my brother and could finally say goodbye to him and close that chapter of my life.

I got rid of many things that day, and as I destroyed each item my heart grew lighter and the depression lifted.

When I completed my spiritual housecleaning, I could tell that something had happened in my heart. I was free from the issues of my past. Within one month the doctors took me off of 10 of those medicines. And I went from being in a psych ward at least twice a month to not going for months at a time. When I look back, I see that getting rid of the things that didn't glorify God was the turning point in my life.

In the following chapters, we'll share other stories of people who put these principles to work and purified themselves of things that held them in bondage. They rid their lives, homes, churches and work places of spiritual darkness and closed trapdoors that the enemy used to gain access to them. Their stories testify to the greatness and power of God and to the authority we believers have in Him to live abundant, free, victorious lives.

Note

1. A pagoda is a tiered tower with multiple eaves common in many parts of Asia. Most pagodas were built for a religious function, most commonly Buddhist, and were often located in or near temples. The modern pagoda is an evolution of the Indian *stupa*, a tomb-like structure where sacred relics could be kept safe and venerated. Pagodas attract lightning strikes because of their height, which may have played a role in their perception as spiritually charged places. Many pagodas have a decorated finial at the top. The finial is designed to have symbolic meaning within Buddhism; for example, it may include designs representing a lotus. The finial also functions as a lightning rod and thus helps to both attract lightning and protect the pagoda from lightning damage. See "Pagoda," *Wikipedia*, March 23, 2007. http://en.wikipedia.org/wiki/Pagoda (accessed March 2007).

CHILDREN AND SPIRITUAL HOUSECLEANING

By now you've noticed that children often experience the effects of spiritual pollution more tangibly than adults do. Cleaning your home of forbidden objects lessens the "attraction factor" to darknes, and opens the door of God's blessing to you and your family. But above all, it brings God glory! Pastor Rene De La Cruz, from California, shared with us the following experience about an anxious father who pleaded for help for his child:

On a cold fall evening in 2002, at about 8 P.M., I was all alone studying in my office. My private line rang, and as I picked up the phone a feeling of dread came over me. In broken English, a man with a Hispanic accent said, "Hello? Is this the children pastor? My baby needs help! Please help my baby!" I could hear a baby screaming in the background.

The man began to tell me that he and his wife had just moved into the area. The couple, their three children, a grandmother and one brother had just moved from Guatemala. He told me that just a few days ago, his one-year-old son began screaming for no apparent reason. He said that the baby had not been able to eat or sleep for about eight days, but the moment they took their child out of the apartment, the baby would settle down, eat and then fall asleep. The couple took the child to a physician and he ran multiple tests. All the tests came back negative—the baby was given a clean bill of health and released.

As the parents walked out of the hospital, a nurse followed them out and whispered to the mother, "Your baby is being harassed by a demon. You must call a pastor." Apparently this man picked up the phone and dialed our church. The man begged for me to come and to pray for his child. I agreed, but first I told him to hold his child in his arms, because I was going to pray for his son. I prayed this prayer over the child, "In Jesus' name, I command this harassing spirit to leave this child alone. I command you to set this child free!" I took down his address and I called Tony, a fellow intercessor.

We pulled up to an old apartment complex and found the unit number. I knocked on the door and the Hispanic gentleman answered and invited us in. Their baby boy lay on the floor, breathing heavily, asleep, and surrounded by the entire family. The father told me that the child fell asleep about five minutes after I prayed for him over the phone.

I felt a spirit of death in the apartment. The man's brother told me that the back room was always cold and that he felt scared every time he was in that room, so scared that he slept on the couch in the living room. As we talked, I asked, "Were there any crimes committed here?" The brother spoke out and said, "Some man was killed here, before we moved in."

Then the grandmother shared stories of lights flickering and strange noises coming from the bedrooms when nobody was home. The two children chimed in with stories of strange shadows that moved around the room.

I told them that Satan looks for opportunities to harass people individually and how territorial spirits will manifest themselves in certain areas where a crime has been committed. But the most important thing that I did was to share the gospel of Jesus Christ. After I shared a bit on spiritual warfare, I told them that they were powerless unless they received Jesus into their hearts. Before I knew it, the mom, dad, children, grandma and older brother all prayed to receive Jesus Christ. It was a divine appointment for sure. Next, we went to every room of the apartment and commanded every foul spirit to leave in the name of Jesus.

The following Sunday the entire family came to church, and to my knowledge the baby and family have not encountered any more strange occurrences in their home.

Isn't it exciting that what the devil intended for evil—to scare and intimidate this family and harass their innocent baby—God turned around and used for good? The enemy's plan was absolutely thwarted when this family not only rid their home of this demonic presence but also (and best of all) gave their lives to Christ.

Spiritual Terror in a Small Tennessee Town

Belinda Dawn Camp encountered a similar type of spiritual terror in 2003 when she and her family lived in a small Tennessee town:

Our family hadn't given much thought to spiritual warfare, until we were spiritually attacked. Some close friends of ours had very recently dealt with the demonic possession of their 18-year-old son, who was into witchcraft. We supported them the best we could, even though we were doubtful and afraid. We'd never experienced this sort of thing, so we weren't sure what to make of it.

Then things began to happen in our home. My young children were frightened, even though we tried to protect them from knowing what was going on. We started to hear loud banging in the walls. We suffered from demonic nightmares. On more than one occasion, my children and I were literally run out of our home by an unseen enemy. The demonic oppression that I felt was the worst feeling I've ever experienced. I didn't know that such a fear even existed. The only way I can describe it is like an invisible wet blanket, drenched in evil, covering me. My thoughts were slow, foggy and didn't seem to be my own. I couldn't concentrate on anything anyone was saying to me.

Gripped with a constant sense of dread and overwhelmed with fear, I couldn't bring myself to break through the oppressive suffocation enough to even pray! Honestly, I was afraid that I might provoke the evil presence to manifest in a way that would literally scare me to death—and that what little faith I had would fail me. It got bad enough that I would awaken to loud, evil chanting but couldn't determine if it was in my bedroom, or simply in my head. For a while I tried to ignore it. I would pretend it wasn't happening and that I was unafraid, but after suffering in utter fear for weeks, I turned for help from our previously mentioned friends and our pastor.

I was given a book to read called *Spiritual Housecleaning* written by Eddie and Alice Smith. It was the same book our friends had read while going through the horrifying ordeal with their son. I was amazed that what I read was right on the mark with what I was going through. I wasn't alone in this feeling! I wasn't crazy! Just reading the book scared me, and for days I could only get past the first few chapters, but when I finished, my eyes were open to the spiritual warfare going on around me. There were things right on the shelf with my Bible that shouldn't have been there that I hadn't given a second thought to! Although we didn't practice witchcraft, we had things like Tarot cards and runes. ("Rune" is a Celtic word meaning secret or mystery.) We had music and books that we shouldn't have had. We even found a toy in my children's room that we had assumed said the Lord's Prayer correctly. Instead, it said "Our mother who art in heaven."

The pastor came and, with the help of our friends, we made a huge bonfire and burned everything that we wouldn't have wanted Jesus to see if He were to show up at our home. It was exhilarating tossing our stuff into the pit. With every trip outside with something to burn, I felt more and more free. Our home felt cleaner. We were ashamed to have had so many things that defiled our home. We rebuked and cast away the demonic spirits in the name of Jesus and then blessed our home. Immediately, the oppression lifted and my family was at ease. I was no longer afraid to be in the house alone! I was no longer afraid to check on my kids in the middle of the night by myself!

Many in our church were doubtful and unsettled about what had gone on in our lives and home. After we shared our ordeal, some members actually left the church, not yet ready to deal with the fact that spiritual warfare is real and was going on in our quiet little town. Although I was sad, I couldn't blame them. I had the same mind before it happened to my family. Still, our pastor was kept busy with the number of people in our church who decided to have a spiritual housecleaning of their own. Many of our church members and friends went out and bought the book for themselves. *Praise God!*

The Battle for Our Children

A spiritual battle is being waged for the souls of our children. Since the beginning of time, this has been the case, but never has the enemy worked so deviously and on so many fronts to destroy a young generation. We really have to consider this battle from two standpoints: the media and our homes.

First, America's homes are under attack and are being invaded by insidious spiritual forces through various media. Evil spirits seek entrance into the privacy of our homes through music, computer images, video games and movies, books, magazines and television shows—many of which can negatively affect our children. Rappers indoctrinate our children to exploit women as sex objects and to have no respect for family, government, God or themselves. Friends tempt them to engage in sexual promiscuity at earlier and earlier ages and entice them with alcohol, nicotine, rebellion, and drugs. Liberal public schools disregard the need for God (we thank the Lord for the godly teachers who continue to stay in these schools). At every turn, godly parents have to be vigilant to successfully contend with the godless world around us.

Even in the godliest home, all it takes is for a child to go to an overnight slumber party with a friend whose father has a stash of porn or whose family subscribes to a cable movie channel and his or her life can be immediately altered forever.

Second, we have spiritually clueless parents who buy Abercrombie & Fitch thong underwear with the word "sexy" embroidered in sequins for their preteen daughters. Parents who buy such things are essentially acting as their daughters' pimps, throwing them to the corporate wolves who will force on them the most lurid, shocking, edgy products imaginable! To some parents, this abdication of parental responsibility is chic. After all, they don't want to appear uptight, overbearing, puritanical or judgmental. They'd rather be their children's friends than their moral compasses and protectors. Parents must wake up and see that America's ugly, shallow, gutter culture is destroying the souls of our children.

Thank God for pastors, churches, specialized ministries and key intercessors who are aware of the spiritual battle we face and who step into the battle as spiritual strategists to provide divine solutions for our children. As parents, we must do the same. Satan takes advantage of every opportunity to steal, kill and destroy. We can't remain naïve to the fact that this is exactly what the devil wants to do to our children and their generation. It's our responsibility to rise up and fight for them—to do everything in our power to see them become powerful men and women who advance the Kingdom of light and not cultural converts who blindly stumble into the kingdom of darkness.

Tools the Enemy Uses to Entrap and Defile Our Children

Satan uses various tools to entrap and defile children. Tereasa Knicely shared the following story with us about the tools the enemy used to defile her children:

One day many years ago, my daughter Sarah was given a Japanese toy by our neighbor who had recently returned from her homeland. It was a strange toy, and I felt that it had some "odd" feelings attached to it.

The next morning, Sarah told me she'd had a strange dream that involved the Japanese toy. It was an evil, eerie dream. I told her that a lot of times Asian toys are made from the idols the Asians worship, such as Buddha, Amitabha, Maitreya, Dharma, Sangha, Krishna, Shiva, Kali, Brahman, Vishnu, Shakti, Ganesh, and others. Evil spirits often stay attached to the idols to keep the seekers deceived. My daughter Sarah understood and without hesitation threw the toy in the trash. No more bad dreams.

Another time, Sarah was playing a *Zelda* video game. *The Legend of Zelda: The Twilight Princess* is part of a popular series of Nintendo video games that involves demons, wizards, ghosts, temples and curses. I watched her play it a few times and then mentioned to Sarah that some of the signs in the game were from the occult and she had better be careful.

She said, "Don't worry, Mom. I can handle it." Over the next six to eight months, however, her anger turned into fits of temper tantrums—at times she ripped holes in our screens and once slammed a door into a wall so hard that the knob went right through it. Right away the Lord prompted me that the *Zelda* video game opened the door, affecting her mind and creating rage in her. I, too, was to blame for allowing my family to have such a game when I felt convicted from the beginning of its occult signs.

I explained all this to Sarah and insisted that she throw it away. I didn't want to give it to anyone else, even though being a collector's edition it had cost me more than $300. Thereafter, I noticed her mind was clearer and her attitude changed. *Praise God!*

As Tereasa points out, toys and video games are at the top of the list of things that can entrap and defile our children. *Why? What could be wrong with toys and video games? They're just child's play, right?* Some are—some aren't!

British author J. K. Rowling has indoctrinated a whole generation of children with the devices of devils through her series of *Harry Potter* books and movies. Unlike some fairy tales where there's a wicked witch who dies because of her malevolence, Rowling's witch is the *central figure of the story!* Harry Potter himself not only lives, he thrives! He's the one who children emulate and bond with. And Rowling's books have collectively sold in the hundreds of millions of copies and have been translated into approximately 50 languages.

Having helped people find deliverance from demonic spirits for almost four decades, we wouldn't expect there to be much immediate demonic manifestation as a result of reading a few books. Not at all. That's just not the modus operandi demons use. They aren't that impatient; they'll manifest later. They typically attach themselves to a person when he or she is young, linger for 10 to 20 years and then, when the person reaches the teen years or adulthood, the demons will surface and systematically destroy the person's life, relationships and influence. Demons are often subtle and shrewd.

When the Battle Begins

The battle begins *before conception* because demonic spirits often move from one generation to the next through what we call generational iniquity. God is a "tri-generational" God—the God of Abraham, Isaac, and Jacob. And Satan said, "I will be like the Most High" (Isa. 14:14). So, Satan works tri-generationally as well.

Generational iniquity is an influence, an open door, or a family trait that's perpetuated in a family as a result of sins committed in previous generations. It causes one to believe and/

or behave in patterns of unrighteousness. Not only do the sins of the parents affect generations to come (Exod. 20:5; 34:5-7; Deut. 5:9; 7:10; Matt. 23:32-36; John 9:2; 1 Thess. 2:16; and 1 Pet. 1:18), but demons that were attached to the parents often move to the children to maintain their grip on the family (Hos. 4:12-13).

Quite often, the battle begins with a preschool child who is sexually molested. For example:

When Joni was five years old, her uncle's wife left him because of his adulterous relationship with one of her friends. When she kicked him out of the house, he moved in with Joni's family for six months. During the night he would visit Joni's room. In her innocence, Joni didn't understand what her uncle was doing to her; and although what was done to her was painful and confusing, she was afraid to tell anyone. Later, when she learned that he had sexually abused her, she was embarrassed to tell anyone.

As Joni grew to adulthood, she found it hard to trust men. She was defensive and frightened around them. However, during her second year in college she met, fell in love with and married a wonderful Christian man. One day during a casual conversation with her father, Joni learned that several of the men on her father's side of the family, like the uncle that molested her, were adulterers and one nephew was a practicing homosexual.

Then Joni realized why her children struggled with their sexual identity. There was an iniquitous pattern that previous generations had established. It had opened the door to darkness in the family. After she and her husband prayed, Joni repented for the sins of her family as Nehemiah repented for his father's in Nehemiah 1:6 and David did in Psalms 106:6-7. Out loud, she broke the attachments to sexual sin and demonic activity associated with her family.

How can one know when the enemy's coming against his or her children?

We often see signs like these with younger children:

- Sleeplessness
- Recurring sickness
- Bad dreams
- Demonic appearances ("monsters in my room")[1]
- Chronic lying
- Excessive fear

Signs of trouble usually exhibited by older children include:

- Rebellion and stubbornness
- Depression or withdrawal (anti-social)
- Verbal abuse
- Anger, temper or rage
- Manipulation or deceit
- Refusal to do household chores
- No interest in formerly productive activities, hobbies or sports

- Trouble at school (suspended, expelled, truant or shows a dramatic drop in grades)
- Trouble with the law
- Experimentation with drugs or alcohol
- Excessive piercings, cuttings, and so forth
- Tattoos of demonic images (gargoyles, dragons, skull and bones, snakes, evil expressions of faces)
- Loss of motivation
- Change in appearance or personal hygiene
- Sexual promiscuity
- Stealing (even from siblings and parents)
- Unwillingness to abide by basic family rules and expectations
- Association with the wrong friends or a bad peer group
- Signs of suicidal thinking

It's possible that your child already owns defiled things. Perhaps you were the one who bought them for him or her. If so, relax. We're all on a learning curve. God is revealing things to us by the day. The very fact that you are reading this book is evidence of your desire to know more about how to please God.

Let's face it: Life's about making midcourse corrections. It's on-the-job training. There are no schools to attend to learn parenting skills. Some people have suggested that if we must have a license to drive, to fish, to hunt and to get married, perhaps we should be required to get a license to have children.[2]

If you've provided unholy things for your children, and the Lord convicts you to confront them about those things, we feel that it's very important that you do this in love and humility.

Explain to your child that you're learning what does and doesn't please the Lord and that the Lord is revealing things to you that the devil might use to harm them. Admit your ignorance in the matter. Apologize. Ask your children to forgive you. Ask them to help you correct the problem in the home. If you learn to apologize to your children when you make a mistake, they are more likely to model the same behavior to you.

Ownership and House Rules

Before we begin, we want you to know that we hold to the principle of respecting ownership. There are two things to consider here: (1) your child (to some degree) owns his or her possessions; (2) you own (to some degree) your child, your home and what's in it. Hopefully you won't have to explain that to your child.

We taught our children that their rooms were in our house. We own the house—therefore, we own the rooms. They use the room, so to speak. They can call a room theirs, but it is completely accessible to us at any time, for any purpose. They don't own the room—we do. With that in mind, we will have final say-so about what is in the room, what is on the walls, what type of music is played there—everything that is done in the room. Once they realize that everything is subject to review, accountability is created in their eyes. Be loving and kind. To be mean-spirited, cruel, rude or abusive to our children is sin and won't produce the desired results.

A note on respecting your child's privacy and property: Unless your child is grossly disrespectful, unmanageable, exhibits self-destructive behavior (e.g., acts suicidal, uses or hides drugs, and so forth) or may be a danger to others, we suggest you not open their journals or diaries. Maintain the right to do so, however, if absolutely necessary.

Rules and limits are necessary for any successful society. It's important that both parents agree to the basic house rules. So, sit down and discuss the issues. As long as the parents can't agree, the child can't be led. If the parents can't agree on the rules, then what they have is a marriage problem, not a parenting problem. They should fix the marriage problem first.

Once that's done, the house rules should be clearly and appropriately presented to the child. The more compliant and responsive your child is, the fewer the rules you'll need. However, if your child is difficult or defiant, you'll need to provide a more defined structure. Control the tone of your voice and maintain a right attitude.

The bottom line? *Responsibility earns freedom. Irresponsibility loses freedom.* Penitentiaries are filled with irresponsible people who've lost their freedom. Tell your children this, and if necessary offer examples so that they are clear about your guidelines. Most important, the house rules must:

- Be clearly communicated and understood
- Be constantly monitored
- Be consistently enforced (learn today that what you say you mean, and mean what you say)

In addition, it's important to have effective consequences that fit the offense. For instance, one young couple came to us concerned because their five-year-old daughter tried to eat the soap at bath time. Deeply distressed over the matter, they explained how one of them had to keep an eye on her every moment during her baths.

Our suggestion? Let her eat the soap.

The mother objected, "No. She'll get an upset stomach."

"Certainly," we agreed. "But she won't eat the soap again."

As you might guess, it worked. The consequences were immediate and effective. (Obviously, this action isn't appropriate if it might endanger your child.)

Another couple came to us because their three-year-old son was impervious to pain. Running in front of a car didn't scare him, and jumping out of a tree didn't faze him. They explained, "He can fall down on the concrete, jump up and continue playing. Nothing hurts him! Even our spankings don't bring tears. We are at our wits' end."

We suggested that rather than spank him, they withhold from him his most prized possession or activity as a consequence of his bad behavior. His favorite activity was art. The next time they had to correct him, they took away all of his crayons and coloring books for 24 hours. He burst into tears. It was punishment enough, and it worked!

Age-appropriate Ways of Dealing with Unholy Possessions

How then do we approach our child concerning things that he or she possesses that are unfit for a young Christian? To a certain extent, this depends on one's opinion, but if our child were 2 years old, we'd deal with him differently from if he were 12 and differently than if he were 16 or older.

Before talking to your child about getting rid of a possession, we suggest you discuss the reasons with him or her why all of us should be concerned about our possessions. Perhaps you could give your child an example of something the Lord asked you to discard. Talk *to* your child, not *down* to your child. Also exercise care that you don't create fear. Children have great imaginations and can be easily frightened. They can become superstitious as well. For that matter, so can parents!

When we taught in Amsterdam several years ago, a lady asked me (Eddie) if she could get demons by picking up her son's dirty clothes. She explained that her older teen wasn't living for the Lord. She obviously thought he was demonized to some degree and was fearful of touching his possessions. The quick answer is, no, you can't. However, if you're this fearful and superstitious, you likely have a hole in your spiritual armor that the enemy could take advantage of (compare Ephesians 4:27 and Romans 14:23 with 1 John 4:18). So avoid being superstitious and creating superstition. It's not mentally, spiritually or physically healthy.

Also, teach your child not to judge others. Explain that because the Lord tells us to get rid of something doesn't mean we are to correct anyone else. We shouldn't attempt to enforce what God reveals to us on others. We're to hear and obey God for ourselves. Trust God to deal with others, but obviously, if someone asks for your advice, you are free to offer it.

The Four General Stages of Childhood

The following are the four general stages of child development: (1) infancy (birth to age 2); (2) early childhood (ages 3 to 8 years); (3) later childhood (ages 9 to 12); and (4) adolescence (ages 13 to 18).

A child's capacity to learn expands as he or she grows through these four stages, and the enemy's approach shifts with each developmental stage.

Dealing with an Infant (Birth to Age 2)

Generally speaking, if your child is an infant, we suggest you remove the questionable object in without drawing attention to it. You might offer a replacement toy. If it becomes necessary to explain, say something like, "Daddy and Mommy felt it was something that made Jesus unhappy, so we put it away. We'll look for something better to replace it." Frankly, it's even better if before you remove it, you offer the shiny new replacement. (Avoid terms such as "devil," "Satan," "demons" and "evil.")

Dealing with a Young Child (Ages 3 to 8)

Children from 3 to 8 years old are all different. Some understand more than others. Until the child is school age, avoid those "hot words" that can produce confusion, curiosity or fear. Instead of saying "devil" or "demons," use the phrase "bad things."

During these years, a child can be taught to respect what he or she has and how to discern whether something should or shouldn't be in his or her possession. When your child is between the ages of 6 and 8, you might even encourage your child to go through his or her own possessions with your help. Hold up each item and ask your child if he or she thinks the object honors or dishonors Christ. Try to make this a happy time; prepare special snacks during break time and read aloud a special prayer of dedication to God once the activity is over. Be creative. Deposit a good memory in your child's "memory bank."

Sherri Weeks from Houston, Texas, shares the following on how spiritual housecleaning affected her two young sons:

After learning about spiritual housecleaning years ago, our family prayed and dedicated our home to the Lord. As we prayed, the Lord revealed specific objects or places in our home that we were to go to. The first place He led us was to our VHS collection of Disney/children's videos. We laid them all out on our couch and prayed over each one. As we came to the movie *Bedknobs and Broomsticks*, the Lord spoke to our eight-year-old son and said to get rid of that now! Our son told us that we should not have this movie—we all agreed, sensing the same thing. We immediately threw it in a garbage bag, prayed and burnt it in a bonfire.

That evening a cool front came in and a good rain. As we cleared the debris from the fire, there were a few things that STILL remained smoldering hot! One was that movie. The Lord showed us the demonic strength of something that we thought was very small and insignificant. As soon as the movie was gone from our home, the tantrums that our young son had been throwing ceased! *To God be the glory!*

When my second son was an infant, he had a bowel obstruction and the doctors couldn't figure out what was causing it or how to help him. A few days after conducting our housecleaning, the Lord took me to the hall closet where I found a book of children's stories that someone had given me. For whatever reason, I had put it away and hadn't opened it.

As I looked through it I had a strange feeling. In the back of the book I discovered that it was published by *Watchtower*. This is the group that publishes the tracks and handouts for the Jehovah's Witnesses. I truly felt that this did not line up with the Word of God. I threw it in the trash and prayed. Within 30 minutes to an hour, my son began a healthy life!

Those are some of the great stories that God has done in our home. We know that He's been faithful to show us the enemy's plans and we know that He will continue to bless us as we seek Him—even in the little things!

Dealing with an Older Child (Ages 9 to 12)

If your child is between 9 and 12 years of age, discuss the issue and explain in more detail the spiritual ramifications of having things that are defiled. You and your child should go through your child's room together. Help your child identify the items, and then help your child research whether or not they are things the Lord wants him or her to have. Find a few Scriptures to read from *THE MESSAGE* or a children's Bible. Give your child the opportunity to get rid of any ungodly objects. If after a few days the items haven't been removed, tell the child that since he or she hasn't done so, you're going to fulfill the responsibility. You might say, "Since we are responsible for the house, we'll make decisions concerning what stays and what goes." You might offer to replace it with something better. You know your children better than anyone, so ask the Lord for a strategy that will please Him.

Dealing with a Teenager (Ages 13 to 18)

If your child is a teenager, do something similar to the above, but if after a few days the items haven't been removed, insist he or she get rid of the items. Explain in a quiet but firm voice that because he or she lives in your home, he or she has an obligation to you. You might say, "We want you to be happy, but until you are old and mature enough to be on your own, we expect the same respect from you that we'd expect from any adult houseguest."

If your teenager doesn't respond appropriately, have a family meeting. Both parents should sit down with the child and explain that since the teen has chosen to disrespect the house rules, an executive decision has been made. *Never lose your temper. Avoid a legalistic attitude and begin your meeting in prayer, asking the Lord for wisdom and understanding.* You might give the teen the opportunity to share his or her feelings. Don't interrupt! At the end, tell your child how much you appreciate his or her openness to discuss an important issue. Then explain that as parents, you are the ones who are ultimately accountable to God. Be open to your child's appeal, and don't be afraid to change your mind about an object if persuaded differently.

As our children became teens, we talked with them as with adults. We still remember with pride how our children did their own spiritual housecleaning. We awoke several times during those years to find sacks of video games, books and articles of clothing outside their bedrooms that they felt the Lord wanted them to discard. In some cases we didn't necessarily feel something was that bad. But it wasn't about us; it was about their conscience and their obedience to God. We respected that and praised them for their sensitivity to the Lord.

Inappropriate Gifts Received from Others

Perhaps the most difficult thing to deal with is when someone gives your child a gift that shouldn't be kept. In this case, it's important not to "lower the bar" and relax the rules. Truth is truth. Don't compromise the truth.

Sheba Daniel sent us the following story about how a gift given by a family member caused unsettling feelings:

> After reading Derek Prince's book *Blessings or Curses You Can Choose* in 1997, I wouldn't let anything that reminded me of the devil into my house. Sometime in 2001, my cousin and her husband came to visit us one day with their baby. They brought a gift for my child—a huge Pokemon™ with a small Pokemon™. At that time, Pokemon™ was very famous, but we didn't know much about it. Seeing the toy itself, however, I felt restless in my spirit. But I didn't want to offend my cousin and her family, so I kept it aside.
>
> Since we live in a one-bedroom apartment, my cousin and her family were given the bedroom to stay for the night, and my husband, my daughter and I slept in the living room. As we were making the bed, my husband told my daughter to take that stuffed Pokemon™ and put it in the kitchen. When I asked him why, he said that he felt the same way as I felt, and he told me that he had no peace in his heart seeing that stuffed animal.
>
> That night we prayed and broke that curse and told the Lord, "As soon as they leave we are going to throw this stuff out." Well, that night, my cousin's baby

couldn't sleep; she cried uncontrollably and they couldn't understand why. They told me that they'd never seen their daughter cry so uncontrollably. We knew why. The next day, after they left, we took the stuffed toys, put them in a bag and threw them into the main garbage of the building.

A few days afterward we saw a program on *The 700 Club* informing us about Pokemon™, how demonic it is, and that it's actually called the "pocket monster." I thank God that the Holy Spirit made us sensitive to this and helped us to throw it out.

Regarding gifts, we suggest two things: (1) don't demean, talk badly about or accuse the giver of wrongdoing; and (2) stress the positives—the giver's generosity and thoughtfulness, for example. Also, make sure that you and your spouse are in agreement before approaching your child. You must stand together in the matter. You can trust the Holy Spirit to guide you with your children—just ask Him!

A Parent's Prayer of Dedication

Heavenly Father, thank You for revealing to us the things in our home that honor You, and the things that dishonor You.

We are grateful to You for giving us the discernment to identify things that would defile our home and the wisdom to take action to protect us.

By faith, we expect to see mighty breakthroughs as a result of our obedience to You.

Now, by the authority we have in Jesus Christ, we dedicate our home, our possessions and our lives to You again.

We declare our freedom from the enemy's plans.
Fill our home with Your glory, Lord Jesus.
Be exalted in our house and our lives as we seek to live totally for You.
In the name of Jesus we pray. Amen.

Notes

1. We believe children are born with the capacity to see the spiritual as well as the natural realm. In time, they tend to grow out of that ability in our society and lose their acute awareness of the spirit world. Why? One reason is because people tend to associate anything like "seeing things that aren't there" with insanity.

2. We are not child psychologists. You may need further counsel to deal with specific problems. If so, see your pastor or another specialist in your area.

SPIRITUAL CHURCH CLEANING

The small Southern church had been on "spiritual life support" for years. Sadly some churches can be in business, yet out of business, and still stay in business! This alone should be enough to cause one to believe in miracles! This was certainly one of those churches. Though located in a thriving neighborhood in a major city, they essentially existed to provide a weekly gathering place for a handful of families and to marry and bury a few folks each year.

The pastor, an evangelist at heart, was dismayed. He'd tried everything he knew to resurrect the little church, yet nothing seemed to work. It was like putting makeup on a corpse. That's when he asked us to bring a team of intercessors to pray through the church property.

Why did he want us to pray through the property? He knew that only God could solve the problem. He also knew that prayer was the key to breakthrough and that God speaks best to those who speak to Him. Intercessors not only speak to God on behalf of others, but God often speaks to them on behalf of others as well.

One Thursday night we gathered about 20 intercessors in the pastor's small building. No one from the church was present, but he'd given us free rein. We worshiped awhile and then began to pray. At one point the Lord impressed us to read the church's minutes. This was a church that held monthly business meetings and, according to the law, had journaled every item of business since the church began in the early 1950s. After considerable study, the team searching through the minutes returned to the group with their report. They discovered the following entry, in the fall of 1958:

> This past week, Jerry Jennings, our new young pastor was killed in a tragic auto accident. *When Pastor Jerry died, the vision of our church died with him.*

In their ignorance, without leadership at the time, the church had pronounced its own death sentence. Why? Proverbs 29:18 says, "Where there is no vision, the people perish" (*KJV*). They had voted to approve the death of the church's vision and recorded it in the legal minutes. It was so.

The Church with a Spirit of Poverty

Tom's church had grown steadily and was now at the point that they needed to move to larger facilities. With much sacrifice on the part of the people, the church bought some acreage in a flourishing part of the city and built a new building. On Dedication Sunday, the building was filled with guests. Many of the members who had fallen through the cracks were back—some they hadn't seen in years!

However, within a few months, to their surprise and disappointment, the church began to experience financial difficulties. They'd assumed that relocating would have launched them to new levels of attendance, participation and ministry. But they were wrong. They now struggled to keep their financial heads above water.

When Pastor Tom came to us for counsel, we asked him if the church had struggled financially like this before. He assured us they hadn't. We asked the pastor how they had procured the land on which they'd built their new building.

Why that question? We asked that because the history of a property often reveals the key to its condition.

Pastor Tom beamed with fatherly pride and said, "We got this land at pennies on the dollar."

"Why was that?" we pressed.

"Well, the previous owners went bankrupt," he explained. We picked up the property for a song."

"Perhaps so," we said, "but you got more than a piece of property. It appears to us that you also got a spirit of poverty."[1]

The previous owners were victimized by a spirit of poverty. They lost the land, and now the spirit of poverty attached to the land was free to move against the new owners.

Too weird, you say?

A Church's Spirit of Jealousy

While conducting a consultation for a large denomination in the United States, one of the denominational leaders shared with me (Eddie) the problem the small church where he was serving as interim pastor was having.

"When this loving church moved into their new building," he said, "all hell broke loose. People became irritable, upset and angry with one another. I don't have a clue what to attribute it to or how to correct it."

I asked him where they got the property on which they built their church. He said, "It was a true blessing of the Lord. Following the death of their father, two brothers fought over ownership of that property for 27 years. Finally, to settle the estate, a judge demanded that they sell the property and split the proceeds. It was a court sale and we got a whale of a deal."

I said, "Brother, you got more than a whale of a deal on a piece of property. It sounds to me like you also purchased a spirit of jealousy, which brings division. You see, the demons that provoked those brothers for 27 years assume that they have rights to the property. Now, unless they're stopped and you purify that property and evict them, they'll provoke you and your members with ongoing anger and division."[2]

Failure to Properly Exercise Church Discipline

Before we ministered to a church in an eastern city in the United States, we briefed our intercessors about why we'd been asked to come and pray over the church's property. The large denominational church was replete with problems of immorality, even at the highest levels of leadership. In fact, they were "pastorless" because their former pastor had left his wife for another woman two years before.

As part of the briefing, we discussed the proper procedure for onsite prayer:

- Keep your eyes open when you pray.
- Look for confirmation from other team members about what you hear the Lord say.
- Don't hold back any direction you feel He gives you.
- Don't war against the enemy without permission from us (the leaders).
- Maintain a spirit of unity. Darkness easily picks up on disunity.
- Pray for direction, discernment and protection.

When we and our team arrived at the large empty facility on Thursday night, a handpicked team of three members of the church ushered us into the pastor's study. No one else was present.

We had the building to ourselves. We briefed the church's team about spiritual things like strongholds and how they can debilitate a church. We explained how the gifts of the Spirit described in Romans 12 and 1 Corinthians 12, when activated and used properly, enabled and empowered our prayer. We outlined several ways God speaks to people through visions (e.g., by giving them a name of a person, an event or even a date or by giving them a sudden feeling of heaviness or lightness), and how the revelation God gives a team member will usually be "in part" (1 Cor. 13:9,12). Why? It's sketchy like this because God wants us to depend entirely on Him. We explained how a team listens and obeys and how the pieces of information soon fit together like the pieces of a puzzle.

We asked the church's team not to mention any details about circumstances or people in the church, unless God brought it to our attention. We try to limit the flesh and allow the Holy Spirit to speak.

I (Alice) shared about defiled land from Psalm 106:32-38. Earlier that day, before we left for the church, the Lord had turned my attention to the book of Jude. (More about that later.) I told the church's team that it was still unclear to me how Jude fit into the picture. Eddie invited the Holy Spirit to lead the team and prayed for darkness to be exposed and for God's light to prevail.

One vision was of a violent confrontation on a staircase leading up to the front doors; another saw the color red.

Another person described an odd-shaped number four. She thought it had to do with small children because of its childlike shape. And there were several other thoughts. With that, the pastoral and intercessory teams discussed the visions.

One of the church leaders shared that there had actually been a confrontation on the front steps of the sanctuary at one time. The front of the building (which we had not yet seen) had a long and steep staircase that led to massive doors. A pastor in the 1950s discovered that the church organist was involved in homosexuality. One Sunday morning, the pastor angrily yanked the young man off of the organ bench, dragged him down the aisle of the church and threw him down the front steps! (Can you imagine this?) It wasn't until we intercessors were taken to the auditorium later that we discovered that there was a "field" of red carpet that led to the platform inside those front doors. Tragically, the pastor who dealt so harshly with the organist was later found to be an adulterer. Sad indeed.

There are two key issues at work here:

1. *Subjective information.* A "word of knowledge" (1 Cor. 12:8) is subjective information. It's the spiritual gift through which God grants supernatural insight and revelation one would not naturally know. Paul said we "seek through a glass darkly" and "we prophesy in part." Because these come in the form of impressions, perceptions and feelings . . . not facts, we rarely act upon subjective information alone.

2. *Objective information.* Objective information consists of historical, verifiable facts, events that actually occurred, people who lived, or history that is already written. These are things that can be validated because facts don't change; they are a solid foundation for effective prayer and the exercise of spiritual authority. Bottom line—facts kick!

A good and balanced intercessory team combines *subjective revelation* with *objective information* and prays to change situations.

The number four, we discovered later, related to an all but hidden area of the church's education facility. It was like a secret attic frequented by children and teens. When we found it, the walls had been freshly painted. The current youth minister had insisted on covering demonic graffiti, including many images that pertain to witchcraft that the church youth had painted on the walls (e.g., upside-down cross, broken cross, pentagram). To our amazement, the odd-shaped number four our intercessor had drawn during our prayer time could still be seen on one over-painted wall. The youth pastor rejoiced that since painting over the symbols, the defiance and rebellion among the youth had decreased. We prayed through the room and awaited our next step.

I (Eddie) felt the Lord say, "The answer is in the bell tower." I asked the church's team if they had a bell tower. Amazed, they said "yes" and they would take us there.

But first, we walked into a baptismal dressing room where three intercessors gasped simultaneously. The three prophetic intercessors perceived that sexual sin had been committed there. The shocked church team concurred and explained that it was where a former pastor and a female church member used to have their sexual rendezvous.

Although I (Alice) spent most of my time interpreting the revelations others received that evening, I too received several significant revelations. One concerned the church's prayer garden. The words "sexual frolic" came to mind as we stood there. The pastoral team said that the garden was known through the years as a place of sexual immorality among some of the members.

I read the book of Jude and, because of what we'd experienced thus far, it was obvious to us why. The circumstances of the book directly related to the circumstances of the church where we were (Jude 4 and 7). I explained to the church's team how to use the book of Jude as a prayer guide for their church. I offered prayer for further revelation and led the group in prayers of repentance on behalf of previous clergy for misleading the church.

We were almost finished when I (Eddie) remembered the bell tower. The church's team led us through the fourth floor to an area that led to the tower. Beyond that door was another flight of very narrow stairs that extended up to the belfry. The belfry was approximately 14 by 14 feet, brick, with small windows. The bell was no longer there. As soon as we stepped into the darkened belfry, I heard an odd fluttering sound. It startled me at first, because of the darkness. I began blindly reaching toward the noise near the floor and cornered and captured a poor, dehydrated, weakened pigeon. It had found its way into the belfry but couldn't find its way out. As I stuck my hand through a cracked window and released it, it glided peacefully to a safe landing in the nearby tree.

It wasn't until then that we remembered, "The answer is in the bell tower." We all concluded that the pigeon was a symbol of the freedom the Lord had brought to the church that night.

At that exact moment, Alice, looking for a light switch, pulled some stage props away from a wall. When she did, there was a noticeable cool breeze that swept across the entire group. Upon examining the space behind the props, it was clear that there was no reason for the breeze—it was a wall. We took it as another sign of the Lord's pleasure (John 3:8).

The teams prayed and blessed the Lord for His revelation and for the freedom the church could now experience. As we moved back toward the pastor's study, we noticed that the atmospheric heaviness had lifted.

When we entered the pastor's study to debrief and offer a final prayer, everyone began to smell something amazing. The closest thing we could think of was the sweet smell of cherry-tobacco pipe smoke. It wasn't distasteful at all. Our first thought was that one of the former pastors had smoked a pipe. But later we realized it was supernatural incense that we smelled—a further sign that the Lord was blessed and the task was completed.

Although no one outside the team members involved knew what we'd done, we can happily report that the church found a godly pastor. Without human intervention, the former pastor repented of his sin and returned to his wife and kids. That was more than 20 years ago. *And they're still happily married.*

Lying (Sinning) to Cover Up Sin

Unfortunately, church discipline is rarely exerted today; and when it is, it is often out of order. In fact, when a pastor or church staff member is dismissed because of sin, many churches hide it. They don't allow the congregation to know what happened. The guilty party leaves, and then the next Sunday, an announcement is read: "Pastor John has felt his assignment here has come to a close. He has offered his resignation effective immediately so that he can find his next pastoral assignment."

Baloney! The deacons and elders sat down with him and he admitted to sexual sin. Rather than repent to the church he has dishonored and resign like a man, and rather than the church leaders telling the members the truth, they lie—adding their sin to his! The result? The church is defiled and thus defeated. The answer? Spiritual church cleaning!

In Exodus 3:5, as Moses curiously approached the burning bush from which God spoke, God warned him to remove his shoes. Why? Because God said, "You're standing on holy ground." The Old Testament refers to defiled land or unholy ground many times. Though many things can defile the land, the following five are the most common:

1. To kill innocent people (abortion, murder) (Amos 1:13; 2 Kings 8:12; Deut. 19:8-12; Isa. 59:3-7; Luke 11:49-51)
2. To worship other gods—idolatry (money, possessions, idols, religious icons) (Judg. 2:1-3; Deut. 12:2-3; 1 Sam. 15:23; 1 Kings 15:11-15; 16:30-33; 2 Kings 17:9-13; 2 Chron. 15:8; Ps. 106:35-39; Ezek. 16:29; Gal. 5:20; Col. 3:5)
3. To commit sexual immorality (adultery, fornication, prostitution, incest, rape, homosexuality, perversion) (Jer. 3:1-2,9; 13:27; Ezra 9:11; Ezek. 23:37-39; Hos. 1:2; Rom. 1:18-32)
4. To break treaties (lies, betrayal) (Judg. 2:1-3; 2 Sam. 21:1-3; Ezek. 5:5-8)
5. To replace the laws of God with man's laws (Isa. 24:5, Jer. 2:7-24)

Our Premise

In terms of ownership, the earth is the Lord's (Ps. 24:1), but any place on earth can either be holy or unholy. The determining factor is what use has been made of the property. Satan has no power of his own—God gave man dominion over the earth. The only power Satan has is given to him through man's sin.

God provided a solution. Christ not only died to reconcile us to God, but also "having made peace through the blood of his cross, by him to reconcile *all things* unto himself; by him, I say, whether they be *things* in earth, or *things* in heaven" (Col. 1:20, *KJV*, emphasis added). Land and property can be cleansed, redeemed and reconciled to God (Lev. 18:24-30). Let's look at two examples of this found in Scripture.

Hezekiah Purifies the Temple

At the end of the eighth century B.C. in Jerusalem, Hezekiah's predecessors to the throne, King Ahaz and other kings before him, had defiled the Temple. Twenty-five-year-old Hezekiah, the new king of Judah and Jerusalem who had a heart to seek the Lord, took it upon himself to cleanse the Temple and make things right with the Lord so that Judah and Jerusalem could again receive God's blessings and protection (2 Chron. 29:1-19).

Notice here that the Temple had been defiled (v. 5). Church buildings can be defiled, just as the Temple was defiled. The Assyrians, the enemies of God's people, defeated Judah, carrying off women and children as captives (v. 9). Likewise, when we open our churches to Satan through sin and defiled objects, family members can be "carried off" and taken captive by satanic forces. Churches grow weak because God removes His presence and His blessings.

How did the Temple become defiled? The "fathers," former kings and Hezekiah's predecessors to the throne, had turned away from the Lord, disobeyed His commands to maintain Temple worship with the order the He'd laid out in the Law of Moses, and had defiled the Temple with abominable objects (vv. 6-7).

So Hezekiah took these corrective steps. First, he renewed the covenant, or commitment, with the Lord (v. 10). Then, under his direction, the priests consecrated and purified themselves (v. 15). They also purified the Temple by removing every unclean thing from it (v. 16). Then the priests returned to the Temple the utensils that God had commanded them to keep there (vv. 18-19). When we purify our lives, confess our sins, repent of and reverse our sinful ways, and remove things from our churches that displease the Lord, we can experience the Lord's peace, His blessings, His favor and anointing.

The result? God was pleased, and His favor returned to Judah and Jerusalem under Hezekiah. This is implied by verse 2: "He did what was right in the eyes of the LORD" (*NIV*).

Idol Feasts and the Lord's Supper

The city of Corinth, referred to in the New Testament, was idolatrous. Demonized worshipers sacrificed animals to their gods. As soon as the sacrifice was complete, they'd carry the carcass to the temple meat market where it would be sold it to people on the streets.

In 1 Corinthians 10:27-29, Paul maintained that eating this meat wasn't a problem unless it caused others to stumble. But there were other Christians who actually participated in the rituals and ate at the temple tables with the heathens (1 Cor. 8). This prompted Paul's warning to Corinthian believers not to frequent heathen temples and eat at their ceremonial tables, and at the same time participate in the Lord's Supper (1 Cor. 10:18-22).

Paul explained to the Corinthian believers that they actually participated with demons when they partook of the food that had been dedicated to the idols (vv. 18-20). Likewise, if we have items or places in our churches that relate to demonic forces or that have been defiled by sin, then we become unwitting participants with demonic forces attached to those defiled objects or places. This provokes the Lord's jealousy over His people. Believe us, you don't want to be on the receiving end of God's jealousy and anger! Often when the Lord was angry with the Israelites, He turned them over to trouble, calamity and defeat at the hands of their enemies. Consider the following passage in Ezra 9:10-11:

> But now, O our God, what can we say after this? For we have disregarded the commands you gave through your servants the prophets when you said: "The land you are entering to possess is a land polluted by the corruption of its peoples. By their detestable practices they have filled it with their impurity from one end to the other" (*NIV*).

This passage makes it clear that the land of Canaan, the Promised Land, had been polluted and defiled by the sins of the Canaanites and then later by the Israelites. Land on which our homes or churches sit can be defiled by our sins or by the sins of previous occupants! This produces the following results:

- *Chain-reaction sin.* Pastoral leaders are gatekeepers (John 10:1-3; Acts 20:28). Gatekeepers open and close the gates to every person and entity approaching the city. In the case of a pastor, what he allows into his own life, he in effect allows into the flock, the church membership. When he sins and his sin is left covered and not dealt with properly, a chain reaction often occurs, just as sin's tendencies are passed to the third and fourth generations from fathers to sons. It is not uncommon that young men and weak Christians fall into sexual sin as a result of a pastor's (spiritual father's) sins. This is what happened in the large denominational church described earlier in this chapter.

- *Public loss of confidence.* Once a church or congregation has been defiled by the misdeeds of its leader, it loses its credibility in the community. First the church stops following its appointed leader. Eventually the community no longer esteems the church and its leaders. The congregation becomes known by the sins of their leader more than for anything else.

- *Spiritual powerlessness.* When sin has been committed in the church and left hidden by leadership, the first one who stops attending the services is the Holy Spirit. He is grieved and no longer manifests His presence.

- *Atmospheric interference.* Oddly, spiritually discerning, godly people will attend one service and be unconsciously turned off. They may not even know why. They simply won't be back. They sensed something wrong and they were unable to attach confidence to the church. This "sense" can sometimes be traced back to past or current sin by church leaders.

- *Relational difficulties.* When the net is broken, the fish escape. When the Body of Christ fails to resolve relational problems, they forfeit many of God's blessings.

When we fail to maintain reconciliation, we cause cracks to form in the foundations of the Church, and relationships erode. Pastor, the longer you ignore and leave relational problems unresolved, the more it will cost you and the church over time. It's usually best to deal with them early and decisively. We're all ministers of reconciliation and should make restitution where necessary (2 Cor. 5:18-19). When we try to convince the world to be reconciled to God (saved), they have every right to ask, "Why would I want to be reconciled to God when you aren't even willing to be reconciled to one another?" Our completion of the Great Commission is based on our unity (John 17:21).

• *Lack of discernment; spiritual blindness.* If we don't act upon things God reveals to us we'll get to a place where He no longer speaks. Light (spiritual discernment and revelation) is given where light is received. This is true of churches as well as individuals.

These are some ways a church's building and property become defiled, its fellowship spiritually crippled, and its ministries compromised.

What to Do If You See These Problems

If you are the pastor of a church with any of these problems, you have a very difficult job ahead of you. This is especially true if it relates to the sins or failings of previous pastors. Why? It may appear that you are simply jealous or that you are pointing to their failures to make yourself look good.

In this position, it's crucial for you to hear the heart of Christ. Remember to balance mercy with justice. It's helpful to have one or more associates that you can partner with in the process. However, they should be well selected, because you will be discussing things that are emotionally charged.

One pastor we love dearly moved too quickly in a situation of this sort and an elderly church couple, who had been in the church for decades, felt threatened, causing the pastor, his family and church great harm. You will need the mind of Christ. Move cautiously and carefully according to God's timetable. What the enemy has taken years to accomplish doesn't have to be overturned overnight.

Precede any corrective action with prayer and fasting. It's usually best made with a small group of committed Christians who are mature enough to deal with these matters. We realize, however, that there are also times when a pastor has to make the move alone, privately.

My (Eddie's) father was once the new pastor of a church that had suffered a church split years before he came. When he found out about it, he scheduled a Sunday evening for his entire congregation to attend the other church's evening service. We entered the other church's auditorium, filled the empty seats and stood around the walls, as my dad walked to the front and asked permission to speak. The gracious host pastor handed him the microphone. My preacher daddy apologized for the actions that had been taken by his church years before he came to pastor it, actions that had helped bring about the church split. The emotional response among both churches was a huge breakthrough for the city. Dad and the pastor became friends, and the churches are at peace with each other to this day.

We've seen pastors assemble a small group of leaders to purify church property. They've used different procedures, as led by the Holy Spirit. We call these "prophetic acts" because they are symbolic of the spiritual truths that are being applied. Here are a few things we've observed:

1. Prayers of repentance for previous sins are followed by prayers of replacement (e.g., "Lord, cleanse us from the sin of sexual promiscuity and make us a people of sexual purity").

2. Oil is dabbed above the doors and windows of the building as each room is dedicated to the Lord.

3. A covenant of love, stating the purpose of the church, is written and the members sign it into the church's legal records.

4. Entire congregations have a night of dedication, signing a document of commitment to God. These services may have repentance, replacement prayers, and prayers of purification and purpose.

5. Groups gather at the four corners of the property and corporately read passages of Scripture and pray prayers of dedication.

6. The building or property is marched around seven times.

7. Scripture is printed, folded or rolled up and inserted into a six-inch piece of half-inch PVC pipe with a cap on each end. One of those pipes is buried the ground at each of the four corners of the property. Oil or wine is poured on each to symbolize purification and dedication.

8. Declarations renouncing the sins—breaking contracts and legal agreements with demons and darkness—and evicting any spirits that are associated presently with the property are read aloud. Then the property is dedicated to the Lord, and freedom is pronounced.

This isn't an exhaustive list, but it includes procedures that have proven powerful. Seek the Lord on behalf of your church and/or church property and ask Him how best to cleanse and dedicate it. Ask Him to speak to you through the Word, through trusted spiritual leaders and through intercessors.

If you're a member of a church that you think needs spiritual cleaning, we suggest that you ponder the need in your heart. Don't share it with anyone, unless he or she is the one who will be directly responsible for correcting the problem (e.g., the pastor). *Pray.* We often say, "Diagnosis doesn't necessarily mean assignment." Just because you have diagnosed a church problem, it doesn't mean you have the assignment to fix it. Prayer is powerful and effective. There may be nothing more for you to do other than pray.

When you feel you have sufficient verifiable information, pray about the right time to bring it to your pastor's attention. When the time comes, make an appointment to meet with your pastor. Be prepared to present your evidence, and be accompanied by witnesses if they exist. Most important, be gentle and humble. Leave the matter with the pastor. He or she is ultimately responsible before God once he or she knows the details.

If you are not a member of the church that you know has been defiled, the handling of the problem depends on the situation. We'll give you two examples.

One day, I (Eddie) received a call from one of our faithful and godly church members. She told me about a nearby church with more than 2,000 members, where she had once been a member. A reliable source had reported to her that this church had been infiltrated by a coven of witches. She went on to describe the situation, including the sacrificing of a cat in the church's prayer room. Her source seemed credible.

The question was what I should do about the situation. I wasn't a member of the church. I was a pastor of another church in the same area. I understood that for me to mention the problem to the pastor could be construed as an accusation against him and his people. I wouldn't want that. So I asked another pastor on our church staff, one with impeccable credentials, to go with me to share what I'd learned. He agreed, and so I made the appointment.

Upon arrival we were cordially received in an elegant office and invited to be seated. I'm sure my heart was beating so strongly that it could be seen through my shirt!

"What brings you fellows here today?" the unsuspecting pastor asked.

I explained that we had good reason to believe that his church had been infiltrated by witches at the highest levels and that a ceremony had been conducted in their prayer room that included the sacrificing of a cat. Frankly, I was prepared for an outburst of disbelief. Instead, he furrowed his brow and quietly said, "Excuse me, gentlemen, I'll be back in a moment." He then left us sitting alone. We looked at each other inquisitively. *What could he possibly be about to do?*

Moments later he returned with several of his staff pastors. "Tell them what you told me," he urged. I did.

Then, one by one, they began to share how the Lord had begun to expose the imposters several months earlier. Three or four of the infiltrators had been removed from top leadership positions. Several were asked to leave the adult choir. The pastoral staff thanked us. They said our visit had confirmed their experiences. Then they asked if we'd go with them to their prayer room for a time of purification. We did.

A different situation called for a different solution. This time we were visiting a foreign country. As we stepped off the plane, we were met by the American missionary who would be our host for the next several days. On the way to his house, he explained how expensive property was and how fortunate they were to have their place of worship.

"Where do you meet?" I (Eddie) asked.

"We meet in the [he named the building]. It's an ideal worship facility. And we almost missed it. You see, another church had it rented on Sunday mornings. So the owner offered us Friday nights. But I investigated and found out how much the other church was paying. I offered the owner more, and he immediately bumped them to Friday night and gave us prime time on Sunday morning. Amazing, isn't it?"

After a few minutes I said, "Pastor, what do we have planned for tonight?" "Nothing at all—you can rest. Why?"

"I'd like to attend church."

"Church? What church?" he asked puzzled.

"The church that meets on Friday night," I explained.

"Why on earth would you want to attend *that* church?" he asked.

"Pastor, we need to attend their church to give you the opportunity to repent to them for taking their worship time. For if you think we're going to stay in your country and minister in your church with this sin hanging over your head, you are sadly mistaken. We'll catch the next plane home."

Needless to say, he was shocked—and convicted. After a few moments of thoughtful deliberation, he humbly agreed.

That night we went to the church, and after we had sat for a few moments, I was able to get the pastor's attention. I said to him, "Pastor, my name is Eddie. I'm from the United States. I have with me the pastor of the church that meets in this facility on Sunday mornings. He is the one who took your Sunday morning worship time from you. He would like to repent publicly to you and your people for doing that. Would you allow us two or three minutes of your time tonight?"

He graciously agreed. And when the time came, he introduced me. I then introduced my host pastor. He stood before the people and sincerely and tearfully repented to them for the underhanded way that he'd treated them. When he finished, I asked, "People, will you forgive this brother for what he's done?" It was a powerful experience that night to be a part of the healing of two churches.

What Should You Expect?

We think you should expect a supernatural response. In the case of the two churches described in the last story, members of both congregations began to meet together for picnics in city parks. They merged some of their ministries, and the pastors preached in each other's pulpits in the months that followed. And over the next two years, both churches tripled in size!

In 1996, David and Maureen Freshour were ministers in West Virginia at a large Baptist church when they were offered the opportunity to come to Washington, D.C. to "restart" a once-thriving church that had fallen into disrepair as the congregation aged and dwindled down to a handful of elderly folks. The Freshours and a team of intercessors prayed for the church, and dramatic events followed:

Rats flee the building or stare you down at your doorway. Roaches that fill the hallway crunch under your feet. Huge black crows line up on your fence and squawk at you. Whoa! Sounds like a scene from a horror flick when the viewing audience wants to scream, "No! Don't go in there!" Many may have thought just that. But the grace of God kept us here.

When we came to Washington, D.C., to "restart" a Baptist church that had suspended its constitution, two statements seemed to sum up the situation we encountered the best: (1) *We knew about the blessings of God but knew little about the activity of the enemy*, and (2) *We didn't have a testimony until we came here*. When you are doing little to oppose the enemy, you encounter little opposition from him. When we accepted the assignment to help this church, little did we know we'd declared war!

Before our start date of April 1, 1997, our former prayer pastor, Marty Cassidy, suggested we attend a spiritual warfare conference in Virginia Beach. This became the foundation that sustained us through the toughest times. We made connections with prayer warriors and mentors who would speak into our lives, pray for us, impart Holy Spirit wisdom and, at times, refuse to confirm what we thought was the Lord calling us out of D.C. In fact, we couldn't get agreement from anyone on that. So we stuck it out.

Although spiritual mapping was new to us, we started to understand that we were a gateway into the city. We are still getting revelation on the importance of our location—the northwest entrance into the nation's capital. We also began to see why the enemy wanted to kill the church and keep it dead. Our spiritual housecleaning became deliberate and desperate. Prayer was focused in our sanctuary, which was unusable and in disrepair. We anointed the church and prayed over it, section by section.

We saw immediate dramatic results. The next day, dead cockroaches filled the hallways. Exterminators parked throughout the neighborhood reported the rats had fled the church. Note that the Holy Spirit was the only "exterminator" we'd invited into the facility! Another time, a rat was sitting on our porch staring at our doorway. Even yelling and stomping didn't move him. We prayed God's blessings over the church and, after we left for a few minutes to go get a witness, the rat was gone. *Rodent terrorists!*

We exterminated many things. We researched church minutes from past business meetings, consultants' reports, library documents, anything to shed light and uncover darkness in the church's past. In the church hallway, former pastors' portraits chronicled the church history. We studied each one: this pastor fell into sin. That one died in a plane crash. This former pastor misspent thousands of dollars. We decided to take down all the pictures.

Fast forward to the year 2000. We hosted the "Glory Fire Conference" for Mike and Cindy Jacobs. When Chuck Pierce came into the pastor's office, he remarked that he couldn't pray in there—it was too dark. Chuck recalled that he had smuggled Bibles into Russia and that it was a dark region of the world, yet our church was the darkest place he had ever been.

Logic didn't rule our actions—we surrendered our reason to the Holy Spirit and operated on raw spiritual instinct. We thought that the house behind the church should be ours, so we prayed for it for three years. It was the oldest house in Chevy Chase, D. C., a very dark, Addams Family-like house. But because God doesn't have to be logical either, He got us the house.

After a dramatic exterior renovation, we unknowingly invited a flock of *huge* crows to our property. They daily objected to our presence. Most birds fly away as you approach—these birds looked at us in defiance, squawking aggressively as we passed. They perched atop the fence that we had to pass to get out the gate into the back of the church. We were "not in Kansas anymore," but felt the same torment that the scarecrow in Oz felt! Two interesting things about crows: (1) To "eat crow" means to retract a statement or admit an error (something we were unwilling to do); and (2) a group of crows is referred to as "a murder of crows" (enough said). We started rebuking the crows. They stopped coming and we haven't seen one since.

The warfare continues, but the spiritual house-cleaning certainly lessened the physical manifestations. While much of our focus was to get rid of the bad stuff, we also made an effort to give away "the good stuff." Pride and selfishness reigned in the former church, so we tried to operate in the opposite spirit. Our facility was crammed with pianos, furniture, pool tables, organs and other valuable "stuff." So we called around and gave it away to struggling churches in the area. When gutting our chapel, the pews went to a new Haitian church. Their members brought their own kitchen chairs each Sunday. How amazing is God?

So where do we stand today? We have opened our doors to many ministries with a desire to be a part of Kingdom work. Our congregation is multiethnic and international, and we minister alongside Korean, Burmese, Panamanian, French African and Ethiopian ministries. We have also been home to Ghanaian, Brazilian, Gypsy and Kenyan congregations that have gone on to larger facilities. Many times, people who visit the city join us for Spirit-led, prophetic worship and then ask if there is a "more Baptist" church nearby. We graciously introduce them to one they might find more comfortable. We take our role as gatekeepers seriously.

We praise God that He's provided people to pray as watchmen with us. We have enormous faith that He who began a good work will be faithful to complete it.

What Does God Expect?

Mark 11:15-17 states, "On reaching Jerusalem, Jesus entered the temple area and began driving out those who were buying and selling there. He overturned the tables of the moneychangers and the benches of those selling doves, and would not allow anyone to carry merchandise through the temple courts. And as he taught them, he said, 'Is it not written: "My house will be called a house of prayer for all nations"? But you have made it "a den of robbers."'"

What does this passage reveal about Jesus' zeal for the house of God? Was He calm and peaceful about it? No! We serve a passionate God who is, as we've noted, jealous for His name's sake and for the pure-hearted devotion of His people. Some things in our churches and on our church property might not seem like sin but might be standing in the way of undistracted worship, and of our entering into the presence of God. As these verses reveal, God will not tolerate the competition!

Let's follow Jesus' example in our churches, our homes, and in our hearts—and wherever we have authority to cleanse and purify a place for His glory. Let's make it our mission to keep His Church clean, to keep it as He desires: *a house of prayer for all nations.*

Notes

1. Not every piece of property bought from a bankruptcy sale has a demonic attachment. Often it is determined by the ongoing sin that is associated with the property.
2. Not every piece of property bought at a court-ordained sale has a demonic attachment or would be considered defiled land. Learning the facts of the case along with unusual activities would be a more accurate way to assess the problem.

WORK, OTHER PEOPLE'S PROPERTY, AND LOVED ONES

Ever felt "slimed" at work—not necessarily by a person, but by the environment itself? Ever wondered why it's hard to concentrate, to communicate, why profits are down, and what to do about profanity, pornography or other offensive material openly displayed in the break room? What's the spiritual climate of your workplace? If it's your own business or if you work from your home, you can easily cleanse your work environment of past sins and lingering foul spirits, but what do you do when you don't have that authority? How can you shed light on a dark atmosphere when it's neither your business nor your building?

What about other people's property? What can you do when your neighbor's behavior is an abomination to the whole street or when you rent a "haunted" hotel room? What kind of action can you take if another person's possessions or property manifest some kind of demonic power that directly affects you?

And what about your loved ones? What if an unsaved family member moves into your home and brings with them spiritual "roommates" of a demonic nature? Or what if a friend or relative gives you or your child a gift that's spiritually offensive? These are hard questions to answer, but the good news is that even difficult situations such as these can be solved with some simple spiritual housecleaning know-how, humility and a heart of faith. The following stories illustrate strategies for dealing with the demonic in your workplace, on other people's property and with your loved ones who don't know any better.

Prayer Changes Everything!

One woman's courage to wield spiritual authority at work led to her promotion and the company's prosperity. She writes:

> I knew it was time to begin looking for a new job. After an interview with this company, I was offered the position. I felt strongly that this was the Lord's will. It seemed like just another chapter in my book of life.
>
> By the end of the first day, I sensed some things very out of order. I went into the break room to heat up some lunch and felt like I had slime all over me. When I turned around to leave, I saw an array of pictures of topless women. I wondered what I'd gotten myself into. I knew that this would have to go or else I would have to go. Knowing that this job was God's will, the choice was obvious. I began to pray against lust, pornography, perversion and anything else I felt the Lord was showing me.
>
> After a couple of weeks, I noticed a strange and unwarranted resentment from the female office manager that I didn't understand at first. As the days progressed

I increasingly felt that something wasn't right with this lady. Things didn't seem to add up. She was often absent, which she said was because she was having difficulty with her pregnancy. I couldn't believe that. Oddly, I prayed against witchcraft and deception although I didn't understand why I felt compelled to pray that way. I prayed that every hidden thing would be brought to the light.

I was bored one day, so I asked my boss if I could reconcile the bank account—which was the office manager's job, but again, she wasn't there. Halfway through the process I realized that there was a check missing that was written for a rather sizable amount. My boss called the bank and they said the check had been written to the office manager. I searched the records for three days without her knowledge and discovered that she'd embezzled almost $20,000 from the company. Everything that was hidden was indeed brought to the light.

She lost her job and I was given her position with a rather nice raise. I still knew I needed to pray through the building and get rid of the demonic activity that I could sense there, but it was difficult to do that at work. I asked the Lord for a time when I could be alone in the building to do spiritual housecleaning.

One day my boss came to me and said the cleaning lady had quit. I offered to clean on the weekends as a part-time job. He liked that idea and gave me a key to the building, which was just what I'd prayed for! I smiled as I knew I would have the building all to myself and could clean it both physically and spiritually.

I came in that weekend and put on some praise music and began with the lunch room. I prayed through all the offices and through the whole building. After only two weeks of praying, the pictures on the wall in the break room were taken down and I hadn't said a word. I praised the Lord and kept pressing in and praying through the building. I began to throw away magazines and catalogs that had occult articles and items in them. I threw away "adult" newspapers every week until they disappeared altogether.

As I first began to take over the accounts as the new office manager, I noticed that we had only enough money to barely get by. I knew that the company had to be blessed in order for me to be blessed. I laid hands on the checks as I printed them, calling in the blessings and commanding the evil to leave. In one year, our sales doubled and we had over $100,000 in the bank, which is good for a small company. The owners of the company recognize that these blessings are from the Lord.

We have had an abundance of work when other shops are laying people off. The entire atmosphere has changed, and it's now both blessed and a blessing. Some people have left, which I know was God's way of purifying, and others have come in that I sense are a link in God's plan for the future of the company. It's a joy to go to work where I know it's my ministry field. We don't have to settle for the atmosphere that we work in, but we can create change if we are diligent to pray, be patient, stay humble and spiritually cleanse our workplace. Greater indeed is He that is in us, than he that is in the world. Change can be a very good thing and the effect can be seen by those around, even if they don't understand the spiritual aspect. We do understand and know who's to receive the glory!

Job Released as House Was Cleared

Sheba Daniel shares the following story about how God opened up an incredible job opportunity in a bank after she cleansed her home from demonic influences:

My husband got a job in the United Arab Emirates. Soon I joined him and began praying for a job for myself.

When I was at home, I listened to recordings of Scriptures about faith. I knew (in a spiritual sense) that my job was already given to me, and I thanked God each day for it; but months passed and I'd not found that job. Then I asked the Lord, "Lord, I know Your promises are sure and they come to pass, but is there anything in me that hinders Your promise from coming to pass? If so, please show me so that I can get rid of it and receive the blessings You have for me."

By this time, I'd had some interviews but hadn't received a call back from any of them. That's when I got a book by Derek Prince called *Blessing or Curse: You Can Choose!* Until that time, I'd never heard that curses could rule a person's life. I thought since Christ redeemed us from the curse of the Law, no curse could come against us. My dad used to tell me, as I put some decorative stuff in the house, that we shouldn't put these images in the house because it would bring a curse, but I didn't believe what he said.[1]

Well, after I read Derek Prince's book, I fasted three days, renounced every curse, confessed things I had done, like going to yoga classes, going to the Hindu temple with my friends and indirectly worshipping their gods, putting their holy water on my head and all sorts of things. Amazingly, the Holy Spirit reminded me about all those one by one—it just came flowing to my mind.

Then I searched my house and threw out rings with demonic designs, silver "good luck" chains, audiotapes, CDs, books and clothes with occult figures on them. I bagged them up and threw them out. I even threw out carvings thinking, "If there is any curse coming into our home through these figures, I'd rather get rid of them." I didn't even want to ask myself whether it was okay to keep this and discard that—I threw out anything that didn't give me peace.

After I did this, I prayed and thanked God. The moment I finished, my phone rang and I was offered three jobs at once. I had difficulty choosing the right one! Finally I chose one and started working and within a month, I was given the best job in the bank!

I learned that it wasn't a lack of faith that held back my blessings; it was a lack of knowledge. Everything changed when I allowed God to move in and teach me what to do, and I obeyed Him. When I go to India now, I am Indian, and buy bed linens, I carefully study the designs on them. Many of those traditional prints have the face or figure of a Hindu god or goddess imprinted on it. I carefully choose the things that I allow to enter my house. If anything doesn't give me peace, I don't let it in. I pray that you'll do the same.

A Coworker Opens the Door to Spiritual Oppression

In our multicultural and religiously diverse society, you hardly know what kinds of spiritual activities your coworkers are involved in. Janell Price shared with us the following story of how a spirit of heaviness (depression) came upon her when she allowed an officemate to predict her future:

About 30 years ago, I took a temporary secretarial job in a small insurance office. Every work day, I ate lunch with one of the lady agents in her office—we were the only two females there.

One day, she took out a pack of cards and casually began telling my fortune. I don't remember that she asked or that I said yes or no. I was so ignorant I didn't know what Tarot cards were.[2] She predicted one thing that happened later that same day. It didn't make me a believer in the occult and I never had another encounter with the occult. But that wasn't because I knew it was of the enemy or against God's Law. I was a born-again Christian who knew very little of the Scriptures.

Sometime later, my husband and I were filled with the Holy Spirit and began going to a wonderful church.

Because I suffered from constant severe depression, I made an appointment with the pastor (Judson Barnwell, then of New Testament Baptist Church, Houston, Texas, now residing in heaven). The heaviness I felt made my life unbearable. Although I had a wonderful husband and two beautiful children, I entertained thoughts of suicide. There was no joy in my life.

Following an opening prayer by Pastor Judson in his office, God gave him a "picture" in his mind of my encounter with the coworker and her Tarot cards. He described to me what he saw and showed me in the Scriptures that I'd violated God's Law and how I'd invited the enemy into my life. I took immediate responsibility for what I'd done, even though I'd done it in ignorance. I was sorrowful that I'd grieved God and I repented. Pastor Judson then took authority over the spirit of heaviness and it left. As I left his office, I noticed that the sun was shining and I felt that life was good. My deliverance was complete and permanent.

In my case, the cleansing of my spiritual house—the one my spirit and soul live in, the one the Holy Spirit lives in—came before the cleansing of my physical house. But the principle was the same: knowing God's truth, lining up with it, and ridding myself of vile things.

It was a life-changing lesson for me. I was struck by how devastating the results of my one encounter with fortune telling had been, even though I had neither sought it, nor had I put faith in it. After I returned home from my deliverance appointment, my husband and I read the Scriptures related to the occult and forbidden objects and went through everything in our home. We threw out things that were expressly forbidden, even things that were doubtful. We gave special attention to our children's possessions, aware of the devastation that can come from so-called innocent involvement. We have continued to stay vigilant from that day to this. We've nothing to do with forbidden things. God's been faithful. The spirit of heaviness hasn't returned (Isa. 61:3).

What Do You Do When It's Not Your Property?

As with church property, demons can inhabit a home, business, or any other kind of land or facility and can, if not properly dealt with, wreak havoc.

An apartment manager in Houston told us, "I dread to see a young happy couple move into apartment 321."

"Why's that?" we asked.

"Every couple that moves into that apartment, no matter the condition of their relationship when they move in, is divorced within a year," she said.

Division lingered in that apartment. An infestation of ants or roaches is bad. An infestation of evil spirits is worse. As soon as these demons of division did their work on one couple, another unsuspecting couple would move in.

Jack York, a different manager, shares how he took his authority in Christ, along with the spiritual housecleaning tools he had learned, to implement *real* home improvement on the property he managed:

I have cleaned house several times, and I believe that it all stemmed from when I heard Alice speak at a convention here in 1996. Alice instructed us to ask God to show us anything in our homes that displeased Him.

I went home and removed everything God told me to remove. Since that time, I occasionally pray through my apartment and ask God to show me anything that isn't right. I also anoint the entrances and I walk outside to pray for everything that I have authority over. I lived in that neighborhood for over eight years and NEVER had my car broken into or my apartment touched. Others in the neighborhood had break-ins in both their vehicles and their residences.

Later I relocated. I was given charge of the grounds to mow and maintain. So, I first prayed over the property and staked out the four corners of the property and claimed it for God. I've prayed numerous times over the house, which was once a roadhouse, and have swept it clean.

When we moved in, I asked God if there was anything I owned that displeased Him. He had me throw out several hundred dollars worth of stuff that a man of God shouldn't have. That was several years ago. Since then, the house has been peaceful. Even when other homes in the neighborhood had been broken into, ours hasn't been touched.

Even though we clean, stuff gets tracked in or allowed in through the telephone, TV or Internet; but when the Holy Spirit brings it to mind, I clean it out and we're at peace. I believe that the enemies of God realize whose property this is and they veer away.

Dealing with Employee Possessions on Your Property

Bob Williams (not his real name) owns a large furniture manufacturing plant in North Carolina. His wife, Loraine, is a wonderful Christian. Bob, now a vibrant Christian, was unsaved when Loraine convinced him to have a team of intercessors come and pray through their business. She told him that it would be good to have the business blessed and to see if the Lord would show the prayer team anything that displeased Him. Bob agreed.

On Thursday night of that week, after business hours and all the employees had gone home, we showed up with our team of intercessors. We first prayed and asked the Holy Spirit to be honored and blessed in this business. Then we explained to Bob and Loraine that we would start at the receptionist's desk and visually investigate the wall hangings, décor and other things in sight. Then we'd pray for discernment regarding the spiritual atmosphere of each employee space.

Perhaps because of Loraine's influence, the offices were fairly clean. Bob was amazed when a couple of the intercessors, hearing from God, began to tell him about some of his former employees. Hearing them describe an affair between two of his former employees "blew him away." The story was true, but Bob was the only one who could have known it. God often shares His secrets with intercessors so that they can pray properly. Information is the fuel of intercession.

When the team moved into the furniture construction area, it was another story. Several of the men had girlie calendars hanging on the walls of their workspaces. The intercessors (mostly ladies) were offended by the sight of them. We suggested to Bob that the calendars with their nude photos dishonored the Lord and were a bad testimony for his business.

Yet unsaved, Bob honored the team's instruction and immediately charged into each space, pulled the offensive calendars off the walls and took them to the trash dumpster! Great, huh?

Not so fast.

You see, the next day when the employees arrived at work and noticed their missing calendars, they lined up at Bob's door to ask him who'd meddled with their stuff. Bob explained that the calendars were inappropriate and that he had removed them. There was quite a bit of tension, which brought Bob to say, "Guys, I'll give each of you some money so that you can go buy a *suitable* calendar for your wall"—which he did.

If you are a business owner, consider doing what Bob and Loraine did and bring in a team to pray through your business. You're responsible for the spiritual atmosphere in your company. You might find that it would settle some of your employee and financial problems.

However, *don't* do what Bob did and destroy property that belongs to someone else. It's true that the men didn't own their workspaces and that, in a legal sense, Bob had the right to do what he did. However, there is a better way. What Bob should have done was call a meeting of the employees to explain to them that he had decided that the calendars would have to go, and why. Then he could have given his employees 24 hours to remove or replace the calendars, or he could have offered to buy them new calendars. In either case, he could then thank them for their cooperation. This would have shown them respect, would have allowed them to do the right thing and would have enabled them to save face in the process.

Dealing with a Family Member Who Defiles Your Home

Sometimes, in tough situations, tough love is required. One woman shared with us the following story about how her mother defiled her home:

> I was born on an island and until the age of 15, I lived with my parents and five other siblings. My dad was going to move to another island to work, and we were moving with him. But my mother could not handle the move, so she moved back home. We children were left with dad.
>
> Over the years, mother would visit us in the U.S., stay with each of us for a while and then go back home. I knew as a child that mother was very superstitious and was often engaged in some sort of ritual, but I thought that that was a thing of the past. I didn't realize that mother hadn't turned from her witchcraft and superstition.
>
> Not too long ago, mother came to visit me. I was excited and began to make plans for her. I wasn't happy with my job at the time and had discussed with mother how evil I thought some of the other

employees were and told her some of the mean things they'd done to me. She suggested that I write each individual's name on a piece of paper. We would cut them into pieces with scissors, and as we did, we would say, "So and so, let evil return to evil."

Sadly, I fell for mother's tricks and witchery. Soon after this episode, I quit my job. It seemed odd that I had put up with the problem for so long, and yet, no sooner had mother come to visit and I quit my job. But I dismissed the thought.

Before this episode, mother told me that she was going to prepare a bath for me. It consisted of coffee, sugar and honey. Rather than show her disrespect, I reluctantly agreed. I didn't bathe in that awful polluted bath water. I discarded it. There was another ritual that she did convince me to participate in. I lit a candle and waved it all around my body and said something that I don't recall exactly. Not once did she use the name of Jesus.

Despite the fact that I reluctantly agreed with mother to do these rituals, I strongly objected to how she adored the moon—especially a full moon. We would sit outside on the patio, taking in the lovely breeze, and she would tell me to talk to the moon and tell the moon how lovely she is and that I love her, and so on. I objected to this, so I would tell her, "No, you're not supposed to adore the moon. It's very unacceptable to the Lord."

Another thing I couldn't stand was the odor of the incense she burned in my house. I asked her to please not do it in the house, so mom would go into our garage to burn incense and conduct her rituals. I noticed that mother's facial features altered during her rituals. She would tie her hair up like someone going to war. I tried very hard to be nice and respectful to her, but when her facial features changed, her demeanor changed. I realized that she was out of control doing her witchcraft while I was at work.

During mom's stay, I became very restless. I'm a busy person normally, but I was becoming confused and unable to concentrate. I was losing control. And when I arrived home from work, I became quite restless. Something was wrong with me, but I could not pinpoint what it was.

Instead of going straight home, many days I would go shopping. In my spirit, I felt something wasn't right at home. Mother would sit in a chair and watch my every move. I could feel an energy drawing and pulling me to her, wanting to control me. I was fighting against it.

One night, as my mother and I sat in the garage, she said, "There is someone out there. Do you hear it?" I heard the wind blow so strongly that it rattled the garage doors. Though it seemed odd, I said, "Oh, mother, there's no one out there! See?" I opened the front door to put her mind at ease, and as strange as this may sound, when I did, I believe demons entered my house. When I went to bed that night, demons were rattling my bed frame, terrorizing me.

I became increasingly restless and confused and unable to sleep well. I also began to feel hopeless, helpless and spiritually defeated. The peace and joy of the Lord had left me.

One night while my mother was gone with one of my siblings, the Holy Spirit showed me that she had brought demonic spirits into my home. When she returned, I unwisely confronted her, lashed out and scolded her. I rebuked her and insisted that she and her demons leave my house. I told her that witchcraft was an abomination to God.

I called my family to tell them that if they didn't remove Mother from my house, I would admit myself into the hospital. She had brought me to the breaking point. After hours of rebuking and commanding demons to leave my house, a calm peace came upon me. That night I slept well for the first time in a very long while.

When I came home from work the next day, my mother was still there. I pressured my siblings to get her out of my house, and they finally came and picked her up. When I gained my composure, I couldn't believe this was happening to me. After all, I'd been a born-again Christian for so long. I even recited the Scripture that no weapon formed against me shall prosper, because greater is He that is in me than he that is in the world. But in reality, I'd let my guard down. It's tragic that I had to deal with my own mother, who was involved in occult practices.

As I studied the Bible and prayed, the Holy Spirit revealed to me that my sorcerer mother had brought the demons inside the house with her witchcraft. I wasn't innocent, because I had participated in mother's rituals, compromising and neglecting my relationship with Jesus. I repented to God for my sin like I hadn't before. The Lord revealed so much truth to me. Day by day my peace, joy and strength returned. God's mercy and grace brought me through this awful experience. I had a new understanding of the spirit world that I'd never had before.

My greatest regret is that out of fear, I didn't handle my mother in a loving, respectful way. At the time, I didn't understand what was happening to me. I should have controlled my anger. When I felt spiritually stronger, about four months later, I had the courage to visit my sister to say goodbye to my mother. She was leaving the States to go back to the islands. I asked for her forgiveness for the way I'd handled the situation. I don't know if she forgave me, but I continue to pray that God will have mercy on her soul.

While this woman couldn't force her mother to change, she could have (and eventually did) enforce the rules of her home—and forced anyone who would not abide by those rules to leave. You have spiritual authority over your home; therefore, you have the right to ask any adult who defiles your home to leave.

The approach will vary from situation to situation, but your first step should be to ask God for guidance and discernment. You might ask another trusted believer to pray both for and with you. Whenever possible, we should employ respect, gentleness and grace when we deal with loved ones (especially older relatives). However, if the other person is belligerent or endangers you or your family, swift and bold (but still God-honoring) action must be taken. Scour your home thoroughly with prayer and praise. Discard or destroy any defiled objects that your former roommate or houseguest may have left behind.

Notes
1. The curse of the Law is a specific curse, which Jesus took upon Himself at Calvary. Our inability to keep the Law would send us to hell, but Jesus took our sin upon Himself, became our righteousness, and fulfilled the law's demand on our behalf. The "curse of the law" has been broken off of us. However, there are other curses of which we should be aware.
2. The Tarot is a set of cards displaying allegorical symbols. Originally used as playing cards, they later came to be used for divination—witchcraft. The cards are divided into Major and Minor Arcana and are used for spiritual, esoteric, psychological, occult and/or divinatory purposes.

SPIRITUAL HOUSECLEANING WISDOM AND WARNINGS

Welcome! You can't imagine how pleased we are to see that you've arrived at chapter 11. Statistics show that of all the people who buy and begin to read Christian books, only a small percentage complete them. You are one of those special few who have fought your way through life's distractions and set aside the time to read this far. You've certainly proved your commitment to assure freedom for both you and your family and to bring glory to God.

We minister around the world in seminars, conferences and other settings. But some of our most favorite and fruitful ministry was when we were pastors. Perhaps that's because we love people and enjoy seeing them move to new levels of spiritual maturity. So we want this final chapter to be a bit more pastoral. If we were your pastors, these are 12 things we would encourage you to keep in mind when conducting spiritual housecleaning or dealing with darkness on any level.

1. Remember Who You Are

If you are born again, you are God's child. Christ is in you, and you are in Christ. God has made you the righteousness of Christ. You don't *do right* to *become* righteous. You *do right* because you *are righteous* (2 Cor. 5:21)!

2. Recognize Your Position

Christ has already won the war against the devil and his demons. Satan's utter eternal defeat is an accomplished fact. Jesus defeated and disarmed him at Calvary. Satan's only two remaining weapons are *lies* and *deception*. Our role at this point is nothing more than a mopping-up exercise. When one army defeats another, the war is over. However, there often remain raids to perform, skirmishes to engage in, and prisoners to take as that victory is enforced. Today, we are enforcing the victory that Christ won at Calvary.

3. Understand Your Rights

You have all the rights of an ambassador. Earth is no longer your true home. Your citizenship is in heaven. You are here on temporary assignment for your King. As His ambassador, you can demand what your King demands, say what your King says and announce the proclamations that your King has made.

4. Operate from a Position of Victory!

Don't operate defensively; operate offensively. Don't respond; initiate! Run to the battle, not from the battle. The devil's gates will not be able to withstand you!

5. Fear Not

Demons are more afraid of you than you could ever be of them. When they see you, they see Christ's glorious life in you, and they're stricken with fear. When you are walking in obedience, filled with His Holy Spirit, they're no match at all for you. Your greatest temptation will most likely be to *fear* them. They take particular pride in seeing us fearful. If we don't fall for that trick, they'll reverse their tactics and tempt us with spiritual pride.

6. Avoid Pride

Never forget that your victories in Christ are His victories. Don't focus on what you've done. Remain focused on who Christ is and what He's done for you, in you and through you. This is the key to maintain your victory.

7. Avoid Superstition

Many Christians who begin to understand the things we've written in this book become "demon-conscious," superstitious, and draw faulty conclusions about things. Remember the following:

- *There are a limited number of demons.* Even if a door has been left open, it doesn't necessarily follow that a demon has taken advantage of it any more than if you leave the door of your house open, a mosquito will *always* fly in.

- *Satan and his demons are not omnipresent.* They can only be in one place at a time. Don't credit them with more than they deserve.

8. Avoid Ritualism

If you submit to superstition, you'll likely give in to ritualism. Spiritual life is based on relationship—not on rituals. There are no silver bullets or magic words when it comes to spiritual warfare. Every assignment and encounter is unique. In every case, we have to depend upon the Holy Spirit.

Sure, we can learn from the experiences of others—both from their successes and from their failures. That's exactly why we wrote this book. But we're not to attempt to duplicate what others have done. Listen to the Holy Spirit before, during and following any spiritual-warfare task. We take orders from King Jesus, the Lord of Host and the Captain of heaven's army!

9. Don't Become Legalistic and Judgmental

Those who fall into *ritualism* become too *legalistic* and are useless in the kingdom of God. Legalistic Christians view themselves as God's police force and rarely win anyone to Christ. No one wants to even be around them, much less be like them. You may have received fresh revelation as you've read this book. Don't mistake that for spiritual maturity. Maturity is not an accumulation of spiritual knowledge, a collection of memorized Scriptures or an understanding of principles. Spiritual maturity is Christ's likeness—God's love and grace operating in us.

Scripture warns us not to judge other men's servants. It's not our job to judge others (i.e., our spouse, friends or pastors). Our job is to love them. The Holy Spirit is their teacher, as He is ours. If you discover that a friend or family member fails to understand important spiritual issues, pray for that person. You can trust God, who revealed the truth to you, to reveal it also to them—in His time. Be gracious. God will not judge them according to His revelation to you; He'll judge them according to His revelation *to them.*

Don't feel compelled to *teach* them. Graciously offer this book to them and leave the matter to God. We provide *information.* Only God can impart *revelation*! So be careful with whom you share issues like these. Careless conversation, especially when laced with pride and legalism, will totally destroy your spiritual credibility, and possibly the relationship.

10. Never Accuse Others

Scripture calls Satan "the accuser of our brethren" (Rev. 12:10). When you accuse, blame or condemn others, you are being conformed to his image! If someone has failed spiritually, it's because Satan has deceived and defeated him or her in the matter. That person isn't the enemy; he or she is the victim. Never lose sight of who the true enemies of your soul are—Satan and his demons.

11. Celebrate Every Victory

Pay attention to the victories you have in Christ. Magnify the Lord. How? Wildly celebrate what He does!

12. Stand

Continue to listen to the Lord for instructions. Some victories are instant; some are progressive. God didn't allow the children of Israel to take possession of all the Promised Land at once. He told them He would give them the land on which they placed their feet. He gave it to them a little at a time, so that they could learn to manage their newfound freedom (Exod. 23:30).

If the warfare continues, it's likely a sign that either God is continuing to train you for an even larger assignment or that you've not yet identified, interpreted and dealt with the defilement correctly. After all, there's more than your life and family at stake here. Nations are hanging in the balance. Be faithful, stand, and expect God's promotion!

CONCLUSION

In Matthew 12:43-45, Jesus says, "When an unclean spirit goes out of a man, he goes through dry places, seeking rest, and finds none. Then he says, 'I will return to my house from which I came.' And when he comes, he finds it empty, swept, and put in order. Then he goes and takes with him seven other spirits more wicked than himself, and they enter and dwell there; and the last state of that man is worse than the first. So shall it also be with this wicked generation."

What do these verses tell us about the power and persistence of the demonic? Does it mean that if you do your spiritual housecleaning, several more spirits will come back and attack you? No, but the devil rarely gives up ground easily. Consider how he tempted Jesus in the wilderness (Matt. 4:1-11), not once or twice but *three times* to get the Son of God to sin. But what's required to keep the atmosphere of your home spiritually clean?

Take some time to examine the spiritual environment in and around your home. Ask the Holy Spirit to reveal anything to you that offends Him and disrupts your home (taking a day or more to pray and fast is a good idea). Then, take note of what God shows you and of what He says to do. If necessary, call in your pastor or another mature believer to help you pray through your home and rid it of any defiled objects. Find favorite Scriptures to declare over your home, then bless and dedicate it as a place of worship, peace, love and holiness—a place under God's authority.

You may want to take a moment to do a quick spiritual housecleaning of your heart and your home by asking yourself these questions:

- What is in my home today?
- Has God shown me one or more possessions in my home that He now wants me to be rid of?
- Are there relationships in my life that dishonor God? What about past relationships? Am I willing to repent and stop these associations?
- Will I turn my heart to hear what God is saying concerning my life, my home and my possessions? Will I obey Him at all cost?
- What about ownership? Am I willing to release ownership of my life, my family and my possessions to Him?
- Have I experienced the cleansing of my home and noticed a positive change in the spiritual atmosphere?

We rejoice with you as you consider these action points. Do what you need to do to gain your freedom. It's often said that knowledge is power. However, that's not true. *Action* is power! Knowing what you've learned is step one. Taking appropriate action is step two. Now step out and do some major spiritual housecleaning!

Closing Prayer

*Father, we pray that You'll grant our readers
with revelation of both Your truth and the
enemy's lies. Reveal any possessions that grieve Your
Holy Spirit and give advantage to darkness.
Bless our friends with the discernment
and discipline to deal decisively with it.
Purify our hearts, our homes, our churches
and our businesses for Your name's sake.
Amen.*

RECOMMENDED RESOURCES

Jackson, John Paul. *Buying and Selling the Souls of Our Children, A Closer Look at Pokemon*. N. Sutton, NH: Streams Publications, 2000.

Jacobs, Cindy. *Deliver Us from Evil*. Ventura, CA: Regal Books, 2001.

Pierce, Chuck. *Protecting Your Home from Spiritual Darkness*. Ventura, CA: Regal Books, 2004.

Prince, Derek. *They Shall Expel Demons*. Grand Rapids, MI: Chosen Books, 1998.

Smith, Alice. *Beyond the Lie: Finding Freedom from the Past*. Minneapolis, MN: Bethany House Publishers, 2006.

_____. *Delivering the Captives: Understanding the Strongman—and How to Defeat Him*. Minneapolis, MN: Bethany House Publishers, 2006.

_____. *Discerning the Climate of the City*. Houston, TX: SpiriTruth Publishing Co., 1997, (800) 569-4825.

_____. *Dispelling the Darkness*. Houston, TX: SpiriTruth Publishing Co., 1998, (800) 569-4825.

Smith, Eddie. *Breaking the Enemy's Grip*. Minneapolis, MN: Bethany House Publishers, 2004.

_____. *Making Sense of Spiritual Warfare*. Minneapolis, MN: Bethany House Publishers, 2008.

_____. *Strategic Prayer: Applying the Power of Targeted Prayer*. Minneapolis, MN: Bethany House Publishers, 2007.

Wagner, Doris. *How to Minister Freedom*. Ventura, CA: Regal Books, 2005.

_____. *How to Cast Out Demons*. Ventura, CA: Regal Books, 2000.

Wagner, C. Peter. *Confronting the Powers*. Ventura, CA: Regal Books, 1996.

_____. *Prayer Shield*. Ventura, CA: Regal Books, 1992.

GLOSSARY

aboriginal: the earliest inhabitants of a region.

Ai: a Canaanite city whose name literally means "a heap of ruins."

amulet: a charm used to ward off disease or evil spells.

angels: immortal spirit beings created by God to carry out His assignments; who operate in different levels of authority (see Eph. 6:12).

apparition: a ghostly figure.

Ark of the Covenant: a large rectangular wooden box overlaid with gold, upon which sat two angels with wings extended (protecting the articles inside), representing God's covenant with man.

artifact: an object produced or shaped by human craft, especially a tool, a weapon or an ornament of archaeological or historical interest.

Asherah poles—*See* **obelisks.**

astrology: the study of the positions and aspects of celestial bodies (through the use of the zodiac) based on the belief that the stars influence the course of human affairs.

Babel: the Hebrew name for Babylon, meaning "to confound."

Babylon: a city created by Nimrod, located in present-day Iraq; considered the seat of Satan, Scripture says it will ultimately be destroyed (see Rev. 14:8; 18).

Beelzebub: a name for Satan; also called the lord of the flies.

brass serpent: the symbol designed by God and made by Moses symbolizing man's insensibility and obstinacy in sin. It was elevated on a pole so that those who were bitten by poisonous serpents that had been sent as a punishment for their murmuring against God and against Moses could be healed (see Num. 21:4-9).

crescent moon: the figure of the moon as it appears in its first or last quarter, waxing (increasing) and waning (decreasing). It has concave and convex edges terminating in points and serves as one of the chief symbols of Islam.

crystal ball: a high-quality clear, colorless glass sphere used by mediums to portend the future.

curses: a calling down of evil or misfortune on someone or something (includes hexes, spells, etc.).

defile: to make unclean, to desecrate or pollute.

deliverance: (exorcism) to expel an evil spirit by command or prayer.

demon: an evil supernatural being; a devil.

demon possession: a term not mentioned in Scripture; Scripture uses the word "demonized," which means to be moved upon or within by an unclean spirit or spirits.

demonized: *See* **demon possession**.

devil: the archangel cast from heaven for leading the revolt of the angels; Satan; the personification of evil and the archenemy of God. Also used to refer to a subordinate evil spirit.

divination: foretelling future events or discovering things using magical powers.

dragon: a spiritual entity described as a gigantic reptile having a lion's claws, the tail of a serpent, wings and scaly skin; a symbol of Satan.

Egyptian ankh: the cross with a loop on top; represents a sex goddess who despises virginity; also a symbol promoting fertility rights, worshiping Ra the Egyptian sun god (Lucifer).

fallen angels: *See* **demon.**

familiar spirit: a demon that communicates with mediums (psychics), those who claim to consult with the dead; a spirit that operates within a family.

fetish: an object which is used to vex the environment with magic powers.

gargoyles: grotesque ornamental architectural figures found on old buildings; they were believed to ward off evil spirits.

geomancy: an Asian system of designing and arranging one's life according to blending of geometry and spiritism, involving some of the theories held by freemasonry.

ghosts: demonic apparitions disguising themselves as spirits of the dead.

heathen: one who adheres to the religion of a people or nation that does not acknowledge the God of Judaism and Christianity.

incantation: a formula of words used to produce magical or supernatural effects; the singing of a spell.

martial arts: any of several Asian arts of combat or self-defense, such as aikido, karate, judo or tae kwon do, based upon heathen deities, usually practiced as sport.

metaphysical: philosophies concerning realities beyond the physical, i.e., spiritual.

Mohammedans, Muslims: adherents of Islam, a monotheistic religion characterized by submission to the demonic god Allah and to Mohammed, his chief and last prophet.

multiple personality disorder: misguided psychiatric diagnosis of the demonic, suggesting that in trauma the human soul splinters into multiple personalities which must be identified, befriended and merged together into one healthy personality.

Native American: a member of any of the aboriginal peoples of the Western Hemisphere whose ancestors are generally believed to have entered the Americas from Asia by way of the Bering Strait sometime during the late glacial epoch. Also called American Indian, Amerindian and Indian.

necromancy: the practice of supposedly communicating with the spirits of the dead in order to predict the future.

New Age: an amalgamation of metaphysical, naturalistic and spiritualist philosophies which call upon spiritual power apart from God.

obelisk: a tall, four-sided shaft of stone, with a pyramid-shaped point. It first appeared in the form of the Asherah pole, used in the worship of Baal and forbidden by God in the Old Testament. It was Asherah (or obelisk) that so infuriated God that He revealed Himself as jealous. (See Exod. 34:13-14; 1 Kings 14:15; 15:13.) It comes from the Hebrew word "asher" which means to erect. It is a symbol of the male phallic and refers to the earth's copulating with the sun. It is a favorite marking stone of Freemasonry. The Washington Monument is the most recognizable obelisk in the United States. It was completed in 1884 and is the tallest masonry structure in the world.

pentagram: a five-pointed star used as a magic symbol.

poltergeist: a noisy, usually mischievous ghost held to be responsible for unexplained noises (such as rappings).

possession: *See* **demon possession.**

rosary beads: a string of beads used for counting prayers in Catholicism; similar prayer beads are also used by other religious groups.

runes: from the Gothic word *runa*, meaning secret, mystery, or whisper. It comes from northern European tribes or Celtic tribes. Runes were used to carve "cursing stones" to defeat intruders.

Satan: *See* **devil**.

Scientology: a rationalistic religion founded by American L. Ron Hubbard; this belief system emphasizes the healing of mind and body by means of following certain rules.

Septuagint: a Greek translation of the Old Testament (c. 300 B.C.).

shaman: an occult priest or witch doctor who uses magic to summon demonic power.

sorcerer: one who seeks to cast spells through incantations, to manipulate spirits or to practice black magic.

soul tie: a spiritual alliance between people that exerts supernatural control over them.

spiritual atmosphere: the prevailing spiritual presence in a region.

stronghold: a fortified place or a fortress.

strongman: the demonic ruler of a stronghold (Matt. 12:29).

superstition: an irrational belief that an object, action or circumstance not logically related to a course of events influences its outcome.

talisman: an object or charm believed to confer supernatural powers, good luck or protection on its wearer.

unholy alliance: *See* **soul tie**.

Unity Church: a religious group that adheres to the doctrine of universal salvation regardless of the beliefs about the death and resurrection of Jesus.

witch: one who seeks supernatural power by practicing sorcery and enlisting the aid of demonic spirits.

witch doctor: an occult priest or shaman who summons demonic power to achieve some particular end.

word of knowledge: a spiritual gift, a manifestation of the Holy Spirit; to possess this gift is to know something beyond natural means through God's revelation (1 Cor. 12:8).

worry beads: a string of beads which the wearer fingers as a form of relaxation or distraction.

vex: to seek to confuse someone by means of a curse.

yoga: a Hindu discipline that seeks to train the consciousness to find a state of perfect spiritual insight and tranquility.

zodiac: a celestial chart representing the paths of the principal planets of our solar system; it is the basis of astrology and is not related to the legitimate study of astronomy. Bottom line: The zodiac, a chart on which all astrology is based, has nothing at all to do with the actual locations of the stars and planets.